Kaplan
Postal Exam
473/473-C

2nd Edition

This publication is designed to provide accurate and authoritative information in regard to the subject matter covered. It is sold with the understanding that the publisher is not engaged in rendering legal, accounting, or other professional service. If legal advice or other expert assistance is required, the services of a competent professional should be sought.

Published by Kaplan Publishing, a division of Kaplan, Inc.
1 Liberty Plaza, 24th Floor
New York, NY 10006

Printed in the United States of America

10 9 8 7 6 5 4 3 2 1

978-1-4195-5311-0

Kaplan Publishing books are available at special quantity discounts to use for sales promotions, employee premiums, or educational purposes. Please email our Special Sales Department to order or for more information at kaplanpublishing@kaplan.com, or write to Kaplan Publishing, 1 Liberty Plaza, 24th Floor, New York, NY 10006.

C O N T E N T S

Chapter 4: Forms Completion (Part B)   29

Chapter 5: Coding and Memory (Part C)   33

Chapter 6: Personal Characteristics and Experience Inventory (Part D)   37

How to Use This Book

Welcome to *Kaplan Postal Exam 473/473-C*, an up-to-date guide designed to help you master the new United States Postal Exam 473/473-C. You may wonder, "How can this book help me in my goal to become a U.S. postal worker?" Here's how!

What Do You Need to Know?

1. *Kaplan Postal Exam 473/473-C* explains the following in clear, direct language:

   ■ Jobs covered by the exam
   ■ How to apply for the exam and when the test dates are
   ■ Kaplan's score-raising strategies
   ■ How to prepare for test day
   ■ What happens after you've completed the exam

2. *Kaplan Postal Exam 473/473-C* provides ample opportunities to practice for Exam 473/473-C with six realistic Practice Tests that will

   ■ familiarize you with what you'll see on test day,
   ■ help you acquire the skills needed to master the test, and
   ■ improve speed and accuracy.

Where to Begin

Begin by reading Chapter 1, which will acquaint you with the details and logistics of applying to take Exam 473/473-C. Next, Chapter 2 introduces the contents of the exam—with examples—as well as some introductory tips and techniques for mastering Test 473.

Chapters 3–6 cover, one-by-one, each of the four parts of the test, including what skills each part tests, how each part is scored, and specific tips for success.

The Practice Tests take about 60 to 90 minutes each to do, including reading directions and completing the unscored coding and memory practice sections (see Chapter 5 for more explanation). Therefore, completing all six Practice Tests will take you about 6 to 9 hours.

You may discover, after taking the first three or four tests, that you need more practice on Part C, for example, and less on Part B. If this is the case, adjust your practicing to focus on the sections you find harder. You may even retake the earlier Practice Tests; there are so many numbers and names in each section, you will have likely forgotten the answers you gave earlier. Remember, however, to time yourself precisely on each of Parts A–D for two reasons: to give real value to your test-taking practice and to relax you for the actual test.

Kaplan Postal Exam 473/473-C offers you the whole package: the research, the contents, the practice, and the strategies you'll require to master U.S. Postal Exam 473/473-C. What you need to add to the mix is your determination to get this job, some sincere concentration, and a few hours of your time. Good luck and let's get started!

CHAPTER ONE

About the 473/473-C Exam

*"What other jobs do you know of with such great benefits,
opportunities, job security, flexibility, and the chance to exercise
right on the job!"*

    —Pat B., U.S. postal worker for 22 years, Altadena, CA

Inside the U.S. Postal Service

On its website, the United States Postal Service (USPS) describes itself as "an outstanding, award-winning service provider for the worldwide movement of messages, merchandise, and money." In fact, the USPS handles over 202 billion pieces of mail each year, thanks to the work of 770,000 career employees serving the American public in about 300 job categories. Tens of thousands of people apply for a variety of USPS jobs every year. These applicants appreciate that USPS employment is interesting; they appreciate that the pay, benefits, and job security are all very good.

    It's probably for these reasons that you have chosen to take one of the USPS entry-level exams, Test 473/473-C (also called the *473 Battery Exam*). Postal Service exams such as Test 473/473-C are open to the public as local staffing needs arise. This entry-level test examines general aptitude and personal characteristics, not knowledge of facts.

Furthermore, Exam 473/473-C serves as a screening process based on job-related skills—such as memory, sorting, coding, and interpreting—allowing applicants (like you!) to compete for positions. Reading this book and taking the six realistic practice exams included herein give you a decided edge over the competition. So let's get started!

Jobs Covered by the 473/473-C Exam

The test is called the *473 Exam* when it is given to fill all entry level jobs in USPS in these areas: Processing, Distribution, Delivery, and Retail. However, because the City Carrier position is the postal job in highest demand, this test is occasionally given just to fill that one job classification. In that event, it is called the *473-C Exam*. Either way, because the exam content is identical, we will usually just refer to it as "Test 473."

Which jobs does Test 473 correspond to? Check out the following positions and their brief descriptions.

City Carriers

City Carriers are full-time career employees who deliver and collect mail on foot or by vehicle, providing customer service in a prescribed area. They sort, rack, and tie mail at the post office before they start making deliveries within their route or area of delivery. They also maintain required information, record changes of address, forward undeliverable-as-addressed mail, and maintain other paperwork. City Carrier applicants must have a current valid state driver's license, a safe driving record, and at least two years of documented driving experience.

Mail Processing Clerks

Mail Processing Clerks are full-time career employees who operate and maintain automated mail-processing equipment or manually sort mail. They collate, bundle, and move processed mail from one location to another.

Mail Handlers

Mail Handlers are full-time career employees who load and unload containers of mail onto and off trucks and perform duties incidental to the movement and processing of mail. Their duties include separating mail sacks to go to different routes or cities; canceling parcel post stamps; and operating canceling machines, addressographs, and fork-lifts. Mail Handlers also open and empty containers of mail throughout the postal facility.

Sales, Services, and Distribution Associates

Sales, Services, and Distribution Associates are full-time career employees who handle direct sales and customer-support services in a retail environment and perform the distribution of mail. The Associates must pass an on-the-job training program.

Basic Requirements for 473/473-C Jobs

General employment eligibility requirements for the USPS are as follows:

Education	There is no education requirement; a high school diploma is not required.
Age	Minimum of 18 years at the time of employment or 16 years with a high school diploma.
Citizenship	Must be U.S. citizen or permanent resident alien.
Language	Basic competency in English.
Selective Service Registration	Males born after 12/31/59 must be registered with Selective Service.
Employment History	Must provide current and 10-year employment history or back to 16th birthday, whichever is most recent.
Military Service	Military service is treated as prior employment; veterans must provide Copy 4 of DD Form 214 and Certificate of Release or Discharge from Active Duty.
Background Check	Local criminal history check is required prior to employment; a more extensive criminal history check is completed at employment.
Drug Screen	Must be free of illegal drugs, which is determined through a drug screen.
Medical Assessment	Conducted to provide information about applicant's ability to physically or mentally perform in a specific position.
Safe Driving Record	Required for employees who drive at work, such as City Carriers and Motor Vehicle Operators.

Specific job descriptions, found online at the USPS website, *www.usps.com,* may also mention job-specific requirements. For example, the listing for City Carrier reads as follows:

- Carriers may be required to carry mailbags that can weigh up to 35 pounds on their shoulders.
- Carriers have to load and unload trays, containers of mail, and parcels weighing up to 70 pounds.
- Carrier duties require prolonged standing, walking, and reaching.
- Carriers work outdoors in all types of weather.
- Most new employees are paid an hourly rate and work a flexible schedule as required by the work flow.

Benefits of Having a 473/473-C Job

As of early 2006, starting wages for entry-level full-time postal jobs ranged from about $14 to $24 per hour. In addition to competitive basic pay rates, most Postal Service employees also receive regular salary increases, overtime pay, night shift differential, and Sunday premium pay.

Besides excellent wages and the attraction of job security, full-time postal employees receive the following benefits:

Health Insurance	Eligible for the Federal Employees Health Benefits Program that provides excellent coverage with most of the cost paid by the Postal Service.
Retirement	Eligible for the federal retirement program that provides a defined benefit annuity at normal retirement age as well as disability coverage.
Thrift Savings Plan	Eligible to contribute to the Thrift Savings Plan that is similar to a 401(k) retirement savings plan.
Life Insurance	Eligible for the Federal Employees' Group Life Insurance Program, where basic coverage is paid for by the Postal Service, with the option to purchase additional coverage.
Flexible Spending Accounts	Eligible for the Flexible Spending Accounts Program, after one year of service, where tax-free FSA contributions can be used to cover out-of-pocket health care and dependent/day care expenses.
Leave	Eligible for a generous leave program that includes vacation leave and sick leave.
Holidays	Postal Service observes 10 holidays each year.

How to Apply for the 473/473-C Exam and Test Dates

So now that you understand some of the requirements and benefits of Test 473 jobs, you probably are curious about the process of applying for those jobs. During this process, you will move through a series of telephone or online steps to see if you are ready and qualified to take Exam 473.

But let's not get ahead of ourselves. To begin the process, you undoubtedly have some questions, such as the following, that you'd like answered.

Why do I even have to take a postal exam? Postal tests are tools the USPS uses to identify which applicants are best suited for particular jobs. In addition, hiring people based upon postal exam scores prevents any form of discrimination.

When are the test dates? There's no simple answer to this question because the USPS does not schedule exams regularly. Each postal district gives the necessary postal tests to fill certain job openings whenever it needs positions filled. Therefore, your first task is to find *an announcement number* for a job opening (or a group of job openings) in the state and town or city where you want to work.

What is an announcement number? An announcement number is a six-digit number that represents one or more jobs in a particular town or city. You'll find job announcement numbers either online at *www.usps.com/employment* or printed on a hard-copy announcement that you may see posted in your local post office or career center.

Online announcement numbers are found in a chart or table. First, you indicate the state you live in and then you scroll down the list by town or city, listed alphabetically. Choose a listing with *Exam No. 473* in the third column. A section of the online chart looks like the following:

City/State	Announcement No.	Exam No.	Exam Title	Opening Date	Closing Date
BAKERSFIELD, CA	145396	932	Electronics Technicians	02/09/10	06/30/10
BAKERSFIELD, CA	145401	933	Maintenance Mechanics	02/14/10	05/30/10
BAKERSFIELD, CA	145408	460	Rural Carrier Associate	03/03/10	06/30/10
BAKERSFIELD, CA	149007	473	Processing, Distribution, and Delivery Positions	05/14/10	08/31/10

BISHOP, CA	145813	943	Automotive Technician	06/07/10	09/30/10
BISHOP, CA	150433	473	Processing, Distribution, and Delivery Positions	06/07/10	10/31/10

Exactly where can I find job announcements? The USPS maintains a national directory or register of job openings. Employment opportunities are listed in several places.

- Online:
  1. Go to *www.usps.com/employment*, or visit the USPS website, *www.usps.com,* and click on the link at the bottom of the page called "Jobs."
  2. Check out listings of federal job vacancies at *www.usajobs.gov*.
- Within the USPS and federal systems:
  1. On public and employee bulletin boards in your local Post Office
  2. On public bulletin boards in Post Office buildings accepting applications
  3. At federal job information centers
  4. In state employment offices
  5. On public bulletin boards in local, federal, state, and municipal buildings
- On public bulletin boards or newsletters:
  1. Colleges and universities
  2. Veterans' organizations
  3. Community service organizations
  4. Community newspapers
  5. Women's and minority associations

How do I sign up to take Test 473/473-C? After you know the announcement number of the job you are interested in, you need to apply for the position, which will also sign you up for the entrance-level exam. *Note that people may only apply during the period the announcement is open and only if they meet the qualifications stated in the announcement.*

Recall that these exams are given to meet the staffing needs of the Postal Service. When the examination announcement is closed (*Closing Date*), applications are usually no longer accepted. If exams are not offered in your area when you are interested, you have two choices:

1. Check back regularly online at *www.usps.com/employment* or by telephone at 1-866-999-8777 (TTY 1-800-800-8776).
2. Choose another state or city that you are willing to relocate to. By the way, you may apply only one time for any one announcement number.

Now that you have your announcement number, you can apply in either of two ways: online or by telephone. The USPS emphasizes: "Due to high call volumes, we recommend you apply online. Applying online will take approximately 2 minutes. Phone applications will take approximately 8 to 15 minutes." Either way, the personal information you provide will be held in confidence—that is the law.

Online   Go to *www.usps.com/employment* and enter the announcement number or search for job opportunities by state. You will be prompted through the application process and asked for other required application information. You will need your full name, Social Security number, street address with ZIP code, and phone number.

If you are selected to take the exam, at least 1–2 weeks before the test date, the USPS will mail you a scheduling package that indicates the exam date, time, and location, along with materials to help you prepare.

For example, the first page you are required to fill out online looks like the following. You are clearly prompted through the remaining pages.

You are applying to take an exam for the following position

Announcement Number: 149007

Examination: 473 Processing,   Distribution, and Delivery Positions

City, State: BAKERSFIELD, CA

To ensure that individuals understand the conditions of the job for which they apply, a series of questions related to the basic requirements for certain entry-level positions with the Postal Service follows. Please read each statement carefully, and then select the appropriate answer for each question, as it applies to you. Your answers will not be used by the Postal Service for making any selection decisions. However, answering "NO" to a question may indicate your lack of interest in the job in question.

Are you willing to work a regular 8 hour shift (plus break time)?	○	Yes
	○	No
Are you willing to work a schedule that may vary from day to day, and may include weekends and holidays?	○	Yes
	○	No
Are you willing to perform physical work, including standing, walking, lifting, and moving objects, for an entire work shift?	○	Yes
	○	No
Are you willing to carry moderately heavy objects (up to 35 lbs.)?	○	Yes
	○	No
Are you willing to lift, carry, or push heavy objects (up to 70 lbs.)?	○	Yes
	○	No
Are you willing to learn to use computers or automated equipment and technology?	○	Yes
	○	No
Are you willing to follow rules and regulations for your personal conduct at work (for example, attendance, smoking restrictions, security requirements)?	○	Yes
	○	No
Are you willing to follow safety related policies and procedures?	○	Yes
	○	No
Are you willing to accept supervision and follow directions/orders?	○	Yes
	○	No
Are you willing to work as a member of a team?	○	Yes
	○	No
Are you willing to cooperate with others in performing work?	○	Yes
	○	No
Are you willing to work with various types of people?	○	Yes
	○	No
Are you willing to develop and maintain positive and respectful working relations with other employees and supervisors?	○	Yes
	○	No
Are you willing to provide service to customers and/or coworkers?	○	Yes
	○	No
Are you willing to keep supervisors and coworkers informed of work-related matters?	○	Yes
	○	No

By phone   To apply on the telephone, call 1-866-999-8777 (TTY 1-800-800-8776) and follow the prompts. The USPS recommends you use a landline touch-tone phone, not a cell phone. You must have an announcement number to apply by phone. You will also need your full name, Social Security number, street address with ZIP code, and phone number.

If you are selected to take the exam, at least 1–2 weeks before the test date, the USPS will mail you a scheduling package that indicates the exam date, time, and location, along with materials to help you prepare.

After you apply for a position, study this book carefully, and then it's time to practice, practice, practice! Remember to arrive early on your test date, carrying the requested materials. Be sure to be well-rested and fueled on a light, nutritious meal. You are ready—you can do it!

What Happens after the Exam?

The National Test Administration Center scores all postal examinations. Results are mailed to all test-takers as soon as scores, job choices, and office choices are available. The process normally takes 4–6 weeks, but this time frame is affected by the number of test-takers. There is nothing you need to do; your results will be mailed to you as soon as they are available.

On all USPS exams, 70 percent correct is the passing score, and 100 percent correct is the top score (not including veteran's preference points, explained in Appendix B). In other words, you need to earn a passing score of 70 on the written examination to continue with the employment process. However, although 70 is the passing score, you'll want to try for 95 percent to 100 percent to have the best chance of being called for employment. The higher your score, the better your chances for USPS employment.

After you pass Test 473, your name is placed on a list ranked by score. As jobs become available, the highest name/score on the list is called in. After one or two years, the USPS discards the old list and builds a new list, and you would need to start the process over again if you are still interested in a postal worker job. However, let's stay positive and work toward passing the test and getting hired for the job you dream of.

To that end, let's look at the composition of Exam 473, along with Kaplan's proven score-raising tips and strategies!

CHAPTER TWO

Kaplan's Score-Raising Strategies

"One of the best parts of my job was watching the children on my route grow up."

Pat B., U.S. postal worker for 22 years, Altadena, CA

An Overview of the Exam

Postal Exam 473 is designed by the Postal Service to test the general and specific aptitudes you need for successful performance in retail, distribution, and delivery jobs, including carrier positions (in which case it's called *473-C*). It tests aptitudes and abilities by having you complete exercises in the types of skills needed to perform those jobs. This book helps you do well on the exam by familiarizing you with the test and the kinds of exercises that are on it. As you learn and practice these skills, your scores will rise dramatically.

Postal Exam 473 tests your ability to accurately and quickly check addresses, complete postal forms, and code delivery routes. You must also be able to remember the correct codes, after an opportunity to look at and memorize them. Finally, you are asked to honestly and accurately assess some of your work-related characteristics and experiences.

The exam consists of the following four parts:

Test Unit	Number of Questions	Time Allowed	Subject Covered
Part A Address Checking	60	11 minutes	Determine if two addresses are alike.
Part B Forms Completion	30	15 minutes	Determine the correct way to complete a variety of forms.
Part C Section 1—Coding	36	6 minutes	Find the correct code to assign to each address.
Section 2—Memory	36	7 minutes	Memorize codes for address ranges and correctly assign them to addresses.
Part D Identify Job-Related Experiences and Characteristics	236	90 minutes	Identify and respond to job-related experiences and characteristics.

Part A: Address Checking

As you can see from the table above, Part A of the test contains 60 items; you will have 11 minutes to mark the correct answers. Each item asks you to compare two addresses, including ZIP codes, and to notice how they are identical and how they are different. The addresses appear in two side-by-side lists: one Correct List and one List to Be Checked. The List to Be Checked may appear identical at first glance to the Correct List; however, it does contain some errors.

Each item in Part A must be answered in one of four ways: *A. No Errors, B. Address Only, C. ZIP Code Only,* or *D. Both*. If the two items are identical, choose *A. No Errors.* If you answer *B. Address Only,* you are indicating that the two addresses differ in some detail of the street address or city and state, but the ZIP Codes are identical. Answer *C. ZIP Code Only* means that one or more numbers in the two ZIP Codes are different, but the street address, city, and state are identical. If there are differences in both of those sections of the address, you'll choose answer *D. Both*.

TRY THIS!

Look at the information in the row below that is labeled **1a.** Compare the **Correct List** to the **List to Be Checked,** and determine whether there are *No Errors (A),* an error in the *Address Only (B),* an error in the *ZIP Code Only (C),* or an error in *Both* the address and the ZIP Code (*D*). In the *Sample Answer Form* below, mark your response by filling in the correct oval. Repeat the process for the rows labeled **2a** and **3a.**

A. No Errors	B. Address Only	C. ZIP Code Only	D. Both

Correct List		**List to Be Checked**	
Address	**ZIP Code**	**Address**	**ZIP Code**
1a. 1841 Chestnut Drive Memphis, TN	38111	1841 Chesnut Drive Memphis, TN	38111
2a. 46 Pistachio Ln Rome, GA	30165	46 Pistachio Ln Rome, GA	39165
3a. 6565 Memorial Blvd Arlington, VA	22213	6566 Memorial Blvd Arlington, VA	21213

Sample Answer Form	**Correctly Completed Form**
1a Ⓐ Ⓑ Ⓒ Ⓓ	1a Ⓐ ⬤B Ⓒ Ⓓ
2a Ⓐ Ⓑ Ⓒ Ⓓ	2a Ⓐ Ⓑ ⬤C Ⓓ
3a Ⓐ Ⓑ Ⓒ Ⓓ	3a Ⓐ Ⓑ Ⓒ ⬤D

The **Correctly Completed Form** shows the correct answers as blackened ovals.

Part B: Forms Completion

In Part B you have 15 minutes to complete 30 items. These items require you to understand various postal forms and to determine where on a form to place certain information. For example, a question might give you specific information and ask where on the form it should be entered, or you may be given a line number from a form and asked what information should go in that section, or you may be asked which of several items could not be placed in a particular box or on a certain line. For each question, you will be given four choices, *A–D,* and asked to blacken the oval on the answer sheet that corresponds to the letter of the correct answer choice.

Study the form on the next page, and then answer the sample questions. In the **Sample Answer Form,** mark your response by filling in the correct oval.

TRY THIS!

1. Last Name	2. First Name	
3. Street Address		
4. City	5. State	6. ZIP Code
7. Action Request (check one) ☐ **7a. Hold mail** ☐ **7b. Return mail** ☐ **7c. Forward mail**	**8. Dates of Action** 8a. From _____ 8b. To _____	

1b. Where should the action request be entered on this form?

    A. Box 2
    B. Box 3
    C. Box 7
    D. Box 8

2b. Which of the following is a correct entry for Line 8a?

    A. 33401
    B. 2006
    C. September 23, 2006
    D. $19.48

Sample Answer Form   **Correctly Completed Form**

1b   (A)   (B)   (C)   (D)   1b   (A)   (B)   ●(C)   (D)

2b   (A)   (B)   (C)   (D)   2b   (A)   (B)   ●(C)   (D)

    The **Correctly Completed Form** shows you the correct answers as blackened ovals.

Part C: Coding and Memory

There are two sections of 473's Part C: a coding section and a memory section. The two sections are related because they use the same codes; but the memory section requires you to memorize the same codes you used in the first section and then to correctly apply them, as you did in the first section.

Section One

Section one of Part C, the coding section, consists of 36 items, in the form of addresses. In addition to the addresses, you are given routing codes, each of which applies to a range of addresses; and you have 6 minutes to assign the correct code to each of the supplied addresses.

Examine the **Guide to Coding** on the next page, and then use it to answer the questions that follow. Notice that a street name may appear twice in the coding guide, but that each time it appears, the street has a different address range associated with it. All addresses within each range run in order from the lowest number to the highest number listed.

TRY THIS!

Guide to Coding	
Address Range	**Delivery Route**
201 – 400 Grinnell Drive 11 – 1000 Sunset Canyon Road **55 – 99 2nd Ave. North**	A
401 – 600 Grinnell Drive 100 – 154 2nd Ave. North	B
12000 – 14000 Constant Sorrow Lane 20 – 70 Rural Route 2	C
Any mail that is not deliverable to one of the above address ranges	D

Sample Coding Questions   Each of the sample questions below consists of an address. Use the **Guide to Coding** above to determine the correct Delivery Route code (A, B, C, or D) for each address. Use the **Sample Answer Form** to record your answers.

	Address	Delivery Route			
1c.	499 Grinnell Drive	Ⓐ	Ⓑ	Ⓒ	Ⓓ
2c.	164 2nd Ave. North	Ⓐ	Ⓑ	Ⓒ	Ⓓ
3c.	34 Rural Route 2	Ⓐ	Ⓑ	Ⓒ	Ⓓ
4c.	350 Sunset Canyon Road	Ⓐ	Ⓑ	Ⓒ	Ⓓ

Sample Answer Form

1c	Ⓐ	Ⓑ	Ⓒ	Ⓓ
2c	Ⓐ	Ⓑ	Ⓒ	Ⓓ
3c	Ⓐ	Ⓑ	Ⓒ	Ⓓ
4c	Ⓐ	Ⓑ	Ⓒ	Ⓓ

Correctly Completed Form

1c	Ⓐ	●B	Ⓒ	Ⓓ
2c	Ⓐ	Ⓑ	Ⓒ	●D
3c	Ⓐ	Ⓑ	●C	Ⓓ
4c	●A	Ⓑ	Ⓒ	Ⓓ

Section Two

After section one of Part C is completed, you will be given 3 minutes to study the coded address ranges you have already worked with in section one. Then you will be required to use those codes, without looking at them, to correctly code 36 more address items.

Look at the **Guide to Coding** and study it for 3 minutes. Then cover it with a blank sheet, return to the questions below, and answer them as quickly and accurately as possible. Use the **Sample Answer Form** to record your answers.

TRY THIS!

	Address	Delivery Route
5c.	12102 Constant Sorrow Lane	(A) (B) (C) (D)
6c.	30 Rural Route 1	(A) (B) (C) (D)
7c.	100 Sunset Canyon Road	(A) (B) (C) (D)
8c.	101 Grinnell Drive	(A) (B) (C) (D)

Sample Answer Form

5c (A)   (B)   (C)   (D)

6c (A)   (B)   (C)   (D)

7c (A)   (B)   (C)   (D)

8c (A)   (B)   (C)   (D)

Correctly Completed Form

5c (A)   (B)   ●C●   (D)

6c (A)   (B)   (C)   ●D●

7c ●A●   (B)   (C)   (D)

8c (A)   (B)   (C)   ●D●

Part D: Personal Characteristics and Experience Inventory

The longest section of Exam 473, as you can see from the previous chart, is Part D. There are 236 items to be completed in 90 minutes. These items are designed to assess several of your personal tendencies and characteristics, as they relate to your work experiences. The characteristics tested are those the Postal Service considers important for effective performance on the job. There is no right or wrong way to answer any item, but the Postal Service has built in methods of catching any attempt to answer in anything other than an honest manner.

There are three sections in Part D. Each section contains items in the form of statements that you should consider in terms of your work, school, or volunteer experiences. The first section has four answer choices, from *Strongly Agree* to *Strongly Disagree*. The second section also has four choices, from *Very Often* to *Rarely*. The third section includes questions that have anywhere from four to nine possible responses.

After reading each item carefully, choose the single response that most accurately describes you in a work situation. Although more than one choice may apply to you, you must choose only one response for each item.

TRY THIS!

1d. You are a methodical worker.
    A. Strongly agree
    B. Agree
    C. Disagree
    D. Strongly Disagree

2d. Despite your best efforts, you tend to argue with others.
    A. Very often
    B. Often
    C. Sometimes
    D. Rarely

3d. What type of work do you like the most?
    A. Fast-paced and varied tasks
    B. Methodical and repetitive tasks
    C. Detailed tasks that can be performed perfectly
    D. Tasks that require considerable use of your own judgment
    E. All of these
    F. None of these

Sample Answer Form						Correctly Completed Form					
1d	(A)	(B)	(C)	(D)		1d	**(A)**	(B)	(C)	(D)	
2d	(A)	(B)	(C)	(D)		2d	(A)	**(B)**	(C)	(D)	
3d	(A)	(B)	(C)	(D)	(E)	(F)	3d	(A)	(B)	(C)	**(D)**	(E)	(F)

Remember, there are no correct answers to any item in Part D, but responses should be truthful.

How to Prepare for Exam 473

There are some general strategies that will lead to your success on Exam 473. You have already taken the first step in buying this book and committing to work through it. Familiarity breeds success, to rephrase an old saying; or, as your teachers used to tell you, knowledge is power. By the time you've finished reading the information in these pages and worked through the exercises, you will be ready to achieve a good score on the exam, one that will qualify you for employment with the Postal Service.

Preparation Matters

One of the primary strategies is to be prepared. Being prepared means familiarizing yourself with the parts of the exam, the question types, and the strategies that will help you correctly answer each question. When you are prepared, you can work quickly and accurately, without wasting any time. It is important to complete all items on the test; and the more you practice, the better you will get at timing yourself and finishing the test. That is why this book contains six complete practice exams.

Where Are the Goal Posts?

To help you attain success on the exam, set interim goals for yourself. Perhaps you can read and digest one chapter of this book a day. Perhaps it will take a week to really master the techniques in each chapter. Your goals should reflect the realities of your schedule. The important thing is to set attainable goals, so that you can meet them and make steady progress. As you begin to feel comfortable with the sections of the exam and as you take the practice tests, your scores will improve.

Decide where and when you will work with the book. You're looking for a time and place you can focus without distractions. For example, if you're a morning person, maybe you can set your alarm a bit earlier than usual and work without any interruptions. You may be very busy, with numerous commitments and responsibilities, but remember—everyone has time he or she can use to accomplish their goals.

Timing Counts

As you take the practice exams at the back of the book, be sure to time yourself. When you take the actual exam, you will be timed; therefore it is vital to get used to the length of each section of the test, so that you will be able to work quickly, answer each item correctly, and get as many points as possible in the time allowed.

One way to pick up a few extra seconds in each section of the exam is to know the instructions for each part so well ahead of time that you don't even need to look at them to know what to do. You will learn what to do by taking the practice exams in this book. When test day comes, you will be ready to open your test booklet as soon as you're given the go-ahead and get right to work, without having to think about what you should be doing.

It can be tempting, when you are in a hurry, to pick the first answer that looks like it might be the right one, so that you can move on to the next question. Resist that temptation! Often, there will be two answers that look pretty good for any given question; and your job is to determine which choice is the best. If you just pick the first answer that could be correct, you will miss many items to which the best answer is *D*.

It can be challenging to complete each section of the exam in the time allowed, even if you never make a mistake that needs to be corrected. So, what do you do when you realize you've made a mistake?

We all make mistakes, and we like to correct our mistakes whenever possible. On this exam, however, there is only one right time to correct mistakes; and that is at the end of each section. Think about it: If you stop to correct an error, you lose momentum, then you have to try to regain your momentum in order to complete the section. Instead of correcting a mistake when you realize you've made one, simply place a tiny mark next to the number of the answer that needs correction. Then, if you finish the section before time is up, go back to each number you marked and correct it. As you work through your practice exams, try this technique; you will see that it works.

Repeat as Needed

Practice makes perfect, so take all of the practice exams in this book. Repetition is an important tool in your preparation program. After you have studied the materials and practiced a full-length test six times, the actual exam will seem almost routine. If you are battling nervousness about the test, thorough preparation is your best weapon, and repetition is the key to staying calm.

Repetition is useful also for memorizing the test instructions as well as the answer choices. By the time test day comes, you will not need to think about reading the instructions, nor will you need to refresh your memory on the answer choices. You will simply know them and be able to spend all your time answering the questions.

As you work, remember that speed and accuracy are what you are striving for. You must work quickly without making errors. In order to do that, you must focus intently on each item as it comes. You cannot allow your attention, or your eyes, to wander. Keeping your concentration going is one skill you must work on as you take the practice exams.

Self-Diagnosis

After each practice exam, evaluate your strengths and weaknesses. Look at each question you missed and determine why you missed it, so that you can avoid making the same type of mistake again. If you are scoring lower on one section than you'd like, analyze the reasons. Perhaps you are reversing some numbers in the ZIP codes, or maybe you need to review the directions for that section again. Once you understand the causes of a less-than-perfect score, you can work on improving your performance.

Success at a Glance

- ■ *Learn as much as you can about the exam*
- ■ *Assess which skills you need to improve for a good score*
- ■ *Set achievable study goals*
- ■ *Practice, practice, practice*
- ■ *Reward yourself for your hard work*

Strategies for Each Section of the Exam

Because different skills are required to master each section of the test, we have different strategies to offer you for each question type. These strategies are as follows.

Part A—Address Checking

In Part A of the exam, you are comparing two lists, each containing an address. You must look at both the street address and the ZIP code to determine if they are identical (answer choice A); if there is a difference, however slight, in the street address only (answer choice B); a difference in the ZIP code only (answer choice C); or if there are differences in both the street address and the ZIP code (answer choice D).

Speed is the key component of this section. It is a test of how many questions you can answer correctly in a given amount of time. Here's how the scoring for Part A works: For each correct answer, you receive one point. Because there are 60 questions in Part A, that is a maximum possible total of 60 points. Obviously, if you don't finish the section, you can't score the maximum number of points. However, if you answer any question incorrectly, a third of a point is subtracted from your point total. For example, if you answered incorrectly on 6 questions out of the 60 you answered, your total score would be 60 minus 2 ($6 \times 1/3$), or 58. If you completed only 55 of the questions and answered 3 incorrectly, your total score would be 55 minus 1 ($3 \times 1/3$), or 54.

It can be tempting to guess at the answers, but you have only a one-in-four chance of answering correctly, and if you guess, and you will lose one-third of a point if you are wrong. Narrow down your answer choices so that you can make an educated guess on each question. If you can't make an educated guess, it might be better to leave an answer blank on this section.

Part B—Forms Completion

Unlike Part A, there is no penalty for guessing on this section of the test. Part B tests your ability to understand and correctly complete Postal Service forms. There are 30 questions, and you have 15 minutes to answer them. Of course, much of your time is spent studying the forms, of which the Postal Service has a seemingly endless array.

As you practice, therefore, train yourself to scan the sample forms for common items, such as name and address. Practice remembering the sections of each form; that way you will be able to spend minimal time looking for a particular type of requested information.

If you can't quickly determine the answer to a question, don't spend much time thinking about it. Place a mark next to the question's number in your test booklet. Then, when you finish the section, return to the marked items and try to eliminate any obviously incorrect answers. If you can narrow your choices, you can make an educated guess. Any time you are able to eliminate a choice, physically cross it out on your test booklet. That way you won't have to look at those incorrect answers again, and you'll save yourself some valuable time.

If you are about to run out of time on this section, be sure to choose an answer for every question. Unlike on Part A, there is no penalty for guessing on Part B.

Part C—Coding and Memory

Part C of Exam 473 contains two sections. The first section checks your ability to correctly code items, quickly and without error. During this section, you are allowed to look at the coding guide while answering the questions. Accuracy is vital during this 6-minute, 36-item portion of the test.

The second portion of the coding section is the dreaded memory test. You must quickly and correctly code 36 more items without the benefit of the coding guide to help you. Fortunately, your score on this section of the exam can be greatly improved with practice and by using a few simple strategies. Essentially, you can train your memory, as you would train your muscles. In Chapter 5 you will learn how to approach memorization in ways that make it both easier and more fun, using images and associations to help you. As with so much of life, success on Part C depends to a great extent on your attitude toward it. Start now to exercise your memory by giving it little workouts in a playful spirit. Instead of having to look up your doctor's address again, come up with associations to help you remember it; instead of using speed dial for the pizza delivery phone number, try to memorize it. You'll find plenty of opportunities to practice memorization—especially if you make up games to test yourself—and then when exam time comes you will be prepared.

There are also a variety of approaches to effectively learning and remembering the codes for Part C. You are given two opportunities to memorize the codes during the exam. These are times when you are not required to work at any task other than memorizing the coding guide. In the chapter of this book devoted to Part C, you will learn the best techniques for memorizing and accurately applying the codes; and the practice tests will give you plenty of opportunity to apply and perfect these techniques.

Remember to apply the same general strategies you use for the other sections of the exam: Make sure you are marking the correct line in your answer booklet, eliminate (and physically mark off) any incorrect answer choices, and mark in your test booklet any items you cannot determine the answer to so that you can return to them later.

Part D—Personal Characteristics and Experience Inventory

The only strategy you need for Part D is to answer the questions honestly—not how you think the test maker wants you to answer them. There are no right and wrong answers for this section, only questions that ask your opinion.

General Preparation Techniques

- Rest up for test day
- Reduce your stress level
- Routine is your friend
- Relax
- Remember to breathe

Rest up for test day   Perhaps when you were in school, you liked to stay up late the night before a big exam so you could cram for it until the last minute. Maybe that strategy even worked for you because adrenaline carried you through the test. But you're probably wiser now, and you know that your brain works better when you are well rested. So, during the week before Exam 473, make sure you get plenty of sleep. It's also a good idea to ease up on your practice schedule because last minute practice-athons only add to your tension.

Reduce your stress level   Easing your tension, in a variety of ways, is the best way to enhance your test performance, as the big day approaches. Here are some suggestions for making sure you are as relaxed as possible on exam day.

Know how to get to the test site and how long it will take you to get there. If possible, make a trial run to the test location. If you're driving, make sure of the route you'll take and know where parking is. Be sure you give yourself enough time to walk from the parking to the exam room. If you're taking public transportation, know when you need to leave and what time you will arrive near the test site. Double-check the correct stop. And remember, it's better to be too early than to be even a little bit late!

Routine is your friend Follow your usual eating and exercise routines during the week before the test. If you aren't used to a particular type of exercise, that week is not the best time to try it out. You don't want to be sore on test day. On the other hand, gentle exercise, or any exercise you are accustomed to, will help you to sleep more soundly and to relax.

Make your last meal before the exam a good one, but not an especially hearty one. A large meal takes blood away from your brain and sends it to your stomach to digest the food. That can make you sleepy and keep you from your best performance.

Relax Speaking of performance, you want to start your preparations for Exam 473 as far ahead of time as possible. That way, you will be confident of your knowledge and ability to perform. But sometimes, no matter how well you prepare, you can still be anxious about the big test day. Anxiety is good to the extent that it motivates you to prepare. As you approach the test itself, however, anxiety stops being your friend. On the test itself, it is your worst enemy.

Humans have a natural "fight or flight" response to anxiety. That response prepares us to defend ourselves or to run away by redirecting blood away from the brain and sending it to our limbs. That response is great for running or fighting, but it's not so good for answering test questions! Your brain will need all the blood you can send it. Therefore, it's important to relax as much as you can during the test.

Remember to breathe One of the most important relaxation techniques is also the simplest: breathe. Most of us like to think that we have a pretty good handle on how to breathe; but the fact is that when you're tense, you tend to forget about one half of the breathing equation, the exhalation. If you're feeling nervous in the exam room as you wait for the test, try breathing in to a count of eight and then out for the same length of time. Repeat. As you focus on your breath, your tension will ease and you will be ready to do your best on the exam.

Address Checking
(Part A)

"Knowing you are providing a vital service to people is an awesome responsibility."

—Pat B., U.S. postal worker for 22 years, Altadena, CA

What Does Part A Test?

Part A of Postal Exam 473, *Address Checking,* tests your ability to quickly compare two lists of addresses, the Correct List and the List to Be Checked, and accurately decide whether they are the same or different. If they are different, you must decide if there is a difference in only the street address or in only the ZIP code or in both the street address *and* the ZIP code.

This part of the test contains 60 items. An item consists of two side-by-side addresses containing either identical or almost identical information. You will have 11 minutes to compare each of the 60 two-address items, determine whether or not they are the same, and mark the correct answers by blackening the corresponding ovals on your answer sheet.

Each item in Part A must be answered in one of four ways: *A. No Errors*; *B. Address Only*; *C. ZIP Code Only*; or *D. Both*. If the two items are identical, choose *A. No Errors*. If you answer *B. Address Only,* you are indicating that the two addresses differ in some detail of the street address or city and state but the ZIP

Codes are identical. Answer *C. ZIP Code Only* means that one or more numbers in the two ZIP Codes are different, but the street address, city, and state are identical. If there are differences in both those sections of the address, you'll choose answer *D. Both.*

Every Second Counts

Eleven minutes isn't very long to answer 60 questions; but, with practice, you can learn to do it. Following are two tips that will save you valuable seconds on Part A:

1. *Memorize the four answer choices. Choice A will always represent* No Errors, *and so on. Confirm your knowledge by taking your practice tests without looking at the answer choices.*

2. *When the proctor says you may open your test booklet to Part A, start answering the first few items in your head. The proctor will give you further instructions; but because you are prepared, you will already know what to do.* **Do not**, *however, pick up your pencil until the proctor says you may begin.*

Speed and Accuracy

It is crucial to correctly identify each error in the List to be Checked. It is also crucial that you practice as much as it takes until you can correctly answer all 60 items in 11 minutes. Remember that test taking is a skill, like any other, and that it improves with repeated practice.

Many people have difficulty answering all 60 questions in the time allowed. If you are one of them, don't worry: just practice. That is the best way to improve both speed and accuracy. Practice gives you the added advantage of feeling relaxed and confident on test day, because you know you're prepared.

How Is Part A Scored?

Part A of Postal Test 473 has a built-in penalty for guessing. Your score consists of the number of items you answer correctly minus one-third of the items you answer incorrectly. In other words, if you answer all 60 items but 9 of your answers are incorrect, you will get credit for only 48 items: your 51 correct answers minus one-third of 9 incorrect answers. You can see that it's better to answer only 51 items than to answer all 60 and get 9 of them wrong.

Fortunately, it is possible to learn to answer each item quickly and with a high degree of accuracy. All you need is lots of practice and a few tips to help you along your way.

Tips for Success

Reduce the chance of error by trying out the following strategies for Part A:

- Learn to focus only on the item you're working on
- Develop a strategy for keeping your place on the answer sheet and in the test booklet
- Break up the addresses into smaller, more manageable pieces
- When you find an error, stop checking that section of the item
- Practice to develop your speed, accuracy, and confidence

Learn to focus only on the item you're working on   This sounds like a simple strategy; but it can be surprisingly difficult when there are distractions in the exam room—and there are always distractions in the exam room, in addition to the fact that test anxiety itself can make it difficult for you to focus.

Practice taking the sample tests in an environment full of distractions. A public situation is best—perhaps you could try working at a public library or in a coffee shop. That is similar to the technique athletes call *overtraining;* that is, you train in conditions that are much more difficult than actual performance conditions, so that you will be well prepared for any challenge that comes your way. Paper rustler behind you? No problem, you'll stay focused.

Develop a strategy for keeping your place on the answer sheet and in the test booklet   Remember to guard against transposition errors. It is a common, horrifying experience to realize when you get to, say, item 49 that you are marking answer number 50 on your answer sheet.

To avoid the disastrous loss of time that results from a transposition error, simply repeat (in your head) the number of each item, both *before* you mark it on your answer sheet, and then again as you mark it. For example, you will focus on number 49, determine that the answer is *A,* then as you turn your attention to the answer sheet, say to yourself "49 is *A.*" You look at the number you're marking —yep, it's number 49. Then, as you turn your attention back to the test booklet, you say to yourself, "49 was *A,*" and now you're ready for number 50. Using this technique, you will never again mark the wrong item number, and your mind will stay completely focused on the item you're working on.

Break up the addresses into smaller, more manageable pieces   Remember that there are two sections to each address: the street address and the ZIP code. The street address has at least two lines: the number and street, and the city and state. That means there are three distinct parts to each address. You will be more successful at finding the errors if you don't try to look at too much information at once. Instead, try breaking each address into its three parts and then comparing each separate part with the List to Be Checked.

As you work, use your pencil (always in your hand, ready to mark your answers) to mark your place on either the Correct List or the List to Be Checked. If you're right-handed, this will probably be the List to Be Checked. Use your index finger on the other hand to mark the corresponding place on the other list. This is also a further example of a technique that helps you focus only on the information that is important at any given moment.

When you find an error, stop checking that section of the item   As you check, for example, the street address, you may notice right off the bat that the street name is spelled differently on the List to Be Checked. Stop right there: There's an error in the address. Don't check the street number; don't look at the city or state. You now know that the correct answer is either *B* or *D*. Move on to the ZIP code and look for an error in it, so that you will know which answer is the right one. Remember, you are working as quickly as possible; when any part of an address is different, the address is different; and you should move on.

You may decide that it is worth it to make a mark in your test booklet any time you answer *A. No Errors* to a question. That way, if you finish early, you can go back and check those items again, to make sure you didn't miss an error. It's more likely that you could miss seeing an error than it is that you would notice an error where there is none.

Practice to develop your speed, accuracy, and confidence   Just as a marathon runner prepares for the big day by running and running some more, a successful U.S. Postal Exam test-taker prepares by taking sample tests and more sample tests. If you haven't met your goals for speed and accuracy after taking the six sample tests in the back of this book, take them again until you do. And while you're at it, convince yourself that there's nothing you'd rather be doing, at least for the moment!

CHAPTER FOUR

Forms Completion (Part B)

*"I enjoyed a variety of tasks and duties in my job—which kept things
interesting at all times!"*

—Pat B., U.S. postal worker for 22 years, Altadena, CA

What Does Part B Test?

Part B of Test 473, *Forms Completion,* tests your ability to identify information
needed to complete forms similar to those used by the U.S. Postal Service. It tests
your common sense rather than your ability to memorize information.

Part B presents several forms used by the U.S. Postal Service. Each box or
blank within a form is labeled; for example, **3** or **4a.** (See the example in Chapter
2.) You will be asked several multiple-choice questions about each form and how
it should be completed; there are usually six questions about each of five forms.
You are given 15 minutes to answer a total of 30 questions, each with four answer
choices: A, B, C, or D. You will need to choose the best answer and blacken the
oval on the answer sheet that corresponds to the letter of your choice.

This second part of Test 473 is quite challenging to test-takers who are not
familiar with postal forms or the items asked for on the forms. You will greatly
increase your odds of mastering Part B by going to your local post office and
picking up one of each of their current forms. Within the six Practice Tests of this

book, you will find fifteen sample forms that are a good representation of the U.S. Postal Service forms. Become very familiar with these forms, and you will find that Part B of Test 473 will be easy to master.

Practice, the Key to Performance!

Practice is the best way to master the forms and to master the skills and speed necessary to assure a high score. Time yourself exactly when you practice, for the following reasons:

1. *You will be heartened by improvements from timing to timing.*
2. *Your practice will be more realistic, like the actual exam.*

How Is Part B Scored?

Your score for Part B of Test 473 is based on the number of items that you answer correctly. **On this part of the exam, there is no penalty for guessing.** It is to your advantage to respond to each item, even if you have to make a random guess. You still have a 25 percent chance of getting the correct answer on a question you don't know. Of course, you have even better odds if you can eliminate one or two of the answer choices, thereby making an "educated guess."

Tips for Success

Reduce the chance of error by trying out the following strategies for Part B:

- Before the test, become familiar with the general directions
- During the test, review each form before responding to the questions
- Look at all the answer choices
- Consider answering items you know now and other items later
- Beware of mixing up letters and numbers

Become familiar with the general directions   The directions to Part B will read something like the following. Become very familiar with these instructions—this familiarity will boost both your confidence and your speed!

> Part B tests your ability to identify information needed to complete various U.S. Postal Service forms. This part of the exam consists of 30 questions to be completed in 15 minutes. You will be shown 5 different forms and be asked to answer 6 items about each form.

Review each form before responding to the questions   Each of the forms in Part B is different. Each of the various sections asks for different information. Take a few moments (not a few minutes) to review each form with care before you begin to answer the questions. Remember, you won't need to know everything about the form, and there will be eight to 30 boxes on each form. You'll need to locate the information or section you are asked about.

Look at all the answer choices   While the U.S. Postal Service is not out to trick you on the exam, you should read each question carefully and study all four answer choices to be sure you didn't take the fast-and-easy answer when a later one was the better choice. For example, the correct answer might be D, an "all of the above" type of answer choice, but you might be tempted to erroneously go for one of the earlier choices (which is correct but not *complete*).

Consider answering items you know now and other items later   However, if you do return to an item later, be sure you mark the correct answer in the corresponding oval on your answer sheet—take care not to lose your place and darken the wrong oval!

Beware of mixing up letters and numbers   Don't be confused by the multiple numbers and letters in Part B. You will be working with lots of figures: question numbers (1–30), answer choice letters (A–D), boxes and lines within each form (such as 3a or 11c), as well as answer choices that might include addresses, ZIP Codes, dates, and route numbers! Just be sure to mark your answers carefully in the correct oval.

CHAPTER FIVE

Coding and Memory (Part C)

*"Postal sorting and reading technology has been modernized to an
amazing degree, depending on the location and size of the post office
you work in."*

—Pat B., U.S. postal worker for 22 years, Altadena, CA

What Does Part C Test?

Part C of Postal Exam 473 actually tests two skills, in two separate sections. First,
it tests your ability to accurately route mail to any address found within a short
list of address ranges by using a Coding Guide to assign the correct route code to
each given item. Then it assesses your ability to quickly memorize those same address range/code pairs, so that you can assign the correct code to an item *without
looking at the Coding Guide*. If you are now deciding that maybe this test isn't
for you, because you often can't remember what you had for breakfast or where
you left your keys last night, please just take a deep breath and prepare to surprise
yourself. Remember that the list of addresses and codes is a short one, and know
that this guide will give you the tools you need for success on this test.

Section One

There are 36 items in Section One of Part C. Most items consist of an address
that could be found within a short list of address ranges. Typically, there are eight

address ranges on the list and four routing codes, A–D. Each address range is paired with one of the routing codes, A–C. Any item that doesn't come from within one of the address ranges should be assigned routing code D. You will have 6 minutes to assign the correct code to each of the 36 addresses.

Section Two

This is the most dreaded section of Exam 473. Section Two of Part C requires you to correctly code 36 more items without looking at the Coding Guide, using only your memory of the Coding Guide from the previous section. You will have 7 minutes to code the 36 items. The good news is that by the time you start answering these questions, you will have already worked with the same address ranges in Section One. Additionally, you will have more time to memorize the address ranges and their corresponding codes; because the exam has both a practice period prior to Section One (which you can use to study, because you will already be familiar with the test) and a formal study period before you begin Section Two.

How Is Part C Scored?

In Part C, as in Part A, you are penalized for incorrect guesses. Your score will be the total number of items you answered correctly minus one-third the number of items you answered incorrectly. Therefore, if you have no idea how to code an item, it is better to not mark any answer; however, in order to succeed on this exam, it is important that you train yourself to answer all items within the time provided. That means it is crucial for you to practice until you can answer every question every time. It also means that you must train your memory—must build it up as you would a muscle—until you can accurately remember the relatively small amount of information you will need to achieve an excellent score on Part C.

Memory Tips

Remember What?

Fortunately, many scientists have spent the past several decades studying how the mind works. They have learned a great deal about how you can improve your memory. Here are some excellent techniques for you to learn and practice.

Visualize   Which is easier to remember: the name Bridgestone, or the image of a giant stone plopped in the middle of a river with cars streaming across it? Cognitive research (the study of how we think) shows that images are much easier for us to remember than words or numbers are, by themselves.

When you learn to quickly make up pictures to aid recall, you will discover that your memory is much better than you ever thought it was. The key to successfully using this technique is giving yourself permission to be silly. Amusing, absurd, even risqué images are the most easily remembered. Human images are especially easy to recall. For example, instead of trying to memorize the range 500–1500 Ellington Drive, imagine the jazz legend Duke Ellington driving a car.

In fact, picture a car and a bus lined up, side-by-side, ready to race. In the car are 5 Duke Ellingtons and in the bus are 15 figures of the musician. Each of the Ellingtons is wearing a colorful shirt with a hundred little pictures of himself on it. Thus, you know that the number range is 500 to 1500 and the street name is Ellington Drive, because Duke Ellington is driving the car and the bus.

Maybe that image doesn't work for you. That's fine, because what makes an image particularly memorable is the fact that it's *your* image. You create it and so you remember it.

Win by association   Another good mnemonic (memory) device is the use of association. If you used to live on Grandview Street, you can easily remember that name in a list of addresses to be coded. If your somewhat nutty dog's name is Chester, you can transform it to help you remember Chestnut Lane. If an address range is on Mercedes Boulevard, you can think of your favorite model of that car. If the numbers within that range are 35–75, think of that as the dollar range you'd pay for the car—in fact, the more ridiculous the association, the easier it is to remember!

The chunkier the better   When it comes to remembering numbers, chunky is good. The best way to remember a list of numbers is to combine or condense them into fewer numbers. The reason for that is the fact that most people can hold only about seven numbers in short-term memory. Some remember as few as five, some as many as nine, but very few can hold more than about seven at a time.

The way to get around this limitation is to chunk numbers together. For example, if you have a string of eight numbers such as 86432006, you can chunk them into four groupings: 86 43 20 06. That's easier, isn't it? Or, you could chunk them into 86 43 2006—even easier.

Remember: get creative

- Unleash your imagination
- Make up an image
- Make an association with something familiar
- Chunk into manageable, memorable pieces

Right the first time   Once you've decided on the particular mnemonic device(s) to use for any given address range, it is especially important that you concentrate on learning the address range correctly the first time. Studies have shown that once a memory trace is formed in your brain, it is difficult to override it. Once you've learned a fact, a number, or an address, it's hard to change what you know. Mistakes tend to remain; so focus, get it right in the beginning, and get a great score.

Tips for Success

1. Prior to showing up for Postal Exam 473, you must first master the format of Part C. That way, you can use the practice time given to you at the

beginning of Section One in order to analyze and start coming up with mnemonic devices for the address ranges.

Before you begin the scored portion of Section One, you will be given time to complete practice questions about the same address ranges that will be used throughout Part C. Simply mark some answers to the practice questions—they will not be scored—then start thinking of images, associations, number chunks, and so forth, for the address ranges.

When the scored portion of Section One begins, concentrate on using the Coding Guide to correctly answer the items listed. Don't worry about memorizing during this time; just answer the questions. If you finish early, go back to memorizing.

2. When the Coding Section time is up, you will begin Section Two, the Memory Section. Again, you will be given time to study and memorize the Coding Guide; then you will answer some practice questions; then you will have another study period before beginning the scored portion of the Memory Section. As you did in the Coding Section, mark some answers to the practice questions, which will not be scored; and then spend the rest of the practice time working on your memorization. When all is said and done, on the test you will have several study periods that add up to almost 10 minutes; and that will be enough time for you to memorize the eight address ranges and their codes, using the mnemonic techniques you have practiced.

3. You are not allowed to write anything down during the memorization periods, but once the 36-question Memory Section begins, you are allowed to write in your test booklet. When you take the practice tests in this book, experiment with writing down the memorized Coding Guide. If that works for you within the time allowed, then follow the same procedure on the exam. On the other hand, you may decide it is better for you just to remember the address ranges and codes.

4. Keep in mind that routing code D is always assigned to any address that cannot be found within the given address ranges. Be forewarned that these addresses are often very similar to ones that could be found within a given range. For example, if there were an address range of 401–690 Mountain Street, you would assign code D to an item such as 400 Mountain Street, 600 Mountain Drive, or 493 Montain Street.

Try This at Home

The more you practice your mnemonic techniques, the better you will be able to use them when test time comes. Practice as you navigate your neighborhood. Try coming up with an image or association for every street, drive, avenue, or circle name you see. Use your imagination, and have some fun.

Take all the practice tests, and if necessary, retake them, until you can achieve a perfect score. Part C may turn out to be your strongest section, the one you can be most confident will help you achieve your goal of a job with the Postal Service.

Personal Characteristics and Experience Inventory (Part D)

"When I took this job, I never expected to be so involved in the lives of so many people. At times I felt closer to my postal customers than my own neighbors, since I saw them more! The clients on my route treated me with respect. It felt like they appreciated the work I did."

—Pat B., U.S. postal worker for 22 years, Altadena, CA

What Does Part D Test?

Part D of Test 473, *Personal Characteristics and Experience Inventory,* assesses the personal characteristics, tendencies, and experiences that would influence your ability to perform effectively as a Postal Service employee. The test items in Part D will cover such issues as dependability, work ethic, performance, productivity, salesmanship, and customer service.

Part D contains items in the form of statements or questions that you react to considering your experiences at work, school, or volunteering. The U.S. Postal Service further emphasizes, "Whenever possible, respond to the items in terms of what you have done, felt, or believed in a work setting." Pick the responses that are *most true about you.*

In Part D—the longest part in the Postal Exam 473—you have 90 minutes to answer 236 multiple-choice items. Some are statements and some are questions, but all refer to *your* personal characteristics and *your* experiences. Don't panic at the number of questions. There are no right or wrong answers here, and the subject matter is *you*.

The Personal Characteristics and Experience Inventory is divided into three segments. The first two segments have a total of 160 test items between them. It's to your advantage to memorize the four set answer choices for these first two groups of statements/questions. However, it is not possible to memorize the answer choices for the third segment, which consists of 76 test items with anywhere from four to nine answer choices each.

1. The first group is the Agree/Disagree segment. There are only four answer choices for this group. An Agree/Disagree item looks like the following:

You prefer to work alone.
A. Strongly Agree
B. Agree
C. Disagree
D. Strongly Disagree

2. The next group of statements and responses is the Frequency segment. There are also only four response choices for this group. A Frequency item looks like the following:

You like to set goals to accomplish a work objective.
A. Very Often
B. Often
C. Sometimes
D. Rarely

3. The third group, the Experience segment, offers anywhere from four to nine answer choices, as seen in the following:

What kind of work do you like the least?
A. Doing the same tasks every day
B. Standing or sitting in one place for hours at a time
C. Moving from task to task quickly
D. Making a lot of decisions
E. All of these
F. Would not mind any of these

How Is Part D Scored?

Your score for Part D of Test 473 is based on an analysis of your responses to the items in this section. The USPS does not explain how this section is scored or how that score affects your overall exam score. However, all responses are considered in determining your results on Part D, so *do not skip any test items*.

Remember, there is no right or wrong way to react to any item in Part D. You might be tempted to select only the responses that seem to make you look your best. However, you must not try to manipulate the answers for this section of Test 473. The Postal Service has incorporated checks and balances into this section to identify a test taker who might be trying to manipulate or "out-psych" the test. Therefore, you'll want to answer as honestly and consistently as possible. Don't waste your time or energy trying to out-psych this section—rather, try to relax, be honest, and be yourself.

Tips for Success

Reduce the chance of error by trying out the following strategies for Part D:

■ Memorize the response choices for the Agree/Disagree and the Frequency segments in advance
■ Read the Experience segment responses with care
■ Mark one and only one response for each item
■ Work at a good clip

Memorize the response choices for the Agree/Disagree and the Frequency segments in advance   While you cannot really "learn" Part D, you can at least become comfortable with the kinds of questions asked and the answer choices for the first two segments. Before you walk into the exam, know both the Agree/Disagree and the Frequency answer choices by heart. They are easy enough to memorize, and then rereading them won't hold you up. You'll just scan the now-familiar responses.

Read the Experience segment responses carefully   A number of questions in the third segment—the Experience section of the test—will offer you answer choices such as the following:

■ All of these
■ Two of the above
■ Two or more of the above
■ None of these
■ Not sure

What Do I Feel?

For some items in Part D, more than one response may describe you or your feelings. Try to respond with the answer that most fits you when you are working. If you cannot relate the question to any experiences in the workforce, consider another experience that may approximate a job, for example, working

■ *in a volunteer position,*
■ *within a club or organization,*
■ *on a neighborhood project,*
■ *in a school theatrical production, or*
■ *on a political campaign.*

KAPLAN

These kinds of answer choices can be confusing! Be cautious in choosing the *most appropriate* of the responses, the one that best fits your experience.

Mark one and only one response for each item   You should evaluate and respond to each item, even if you are not completely sure which choice is best. It is vital to your success in Part D that you mark only one answer for each item. There will be some statements or questions where more than one answer choice seems appropriate. Nevertheless, choose only one—the one that applies most closely to your work experiences. Please remember, do not attempt to distort or shape your self-descriptions on this test—just be honest and consistent in marking the answer that best describes your personal opinion.

Work at a good clip   Part D is probably best completed at a fairly rapid pace. Your natural tendency may be to overevaluate each statement or to reconsider your feelings and reactions with similar test items. Don't be tempted to over-evaluate; just react.

With 236 items to complete in 90 minutes, you should be *averaging* between 2½ and 3 questions a minute. However, note that you will move through the Agree/Disagree and the Frequency segments much more quickly than the Experience segment because those first two sections have only four set answer choices for each item—and you will have memorized those choices by the exam date. The Experience segment will naturally take longer because there are four to nine original answer choices for each item—none of which can be memorized in advance.

The USPS usually allows test-takers to leave if they have finished this last part of Test 473 before time is called. Most people do finish before the 90 minutes are up, so don't worry about the time limit on Part D.

Try to relax and actually enjoy this part of Postal Exam 473. In Part D there are no right or wrong answers and it is all about you!

How to Use the Answer Sheets

At the beginning of each practice test, you will find answer sheets to use in taking the tests. These are similar to the answer sheets you will be provided when you take the actual Postal Exam.

Tear out or photocopy an answer sheet before you begin a practice test, and use it to record your answers. Mark your answer to each question by filling in the oval that contains the letter corresponding to the correct answer.

You will notice that there are no questions for Part D in any of the practice exams. That is because, as has been explained in this book, Part D is composed of 236 statements and questions that are impossible to prepare for—except for familiarizing yourself with the types of questions that will be asked and the categories of responses that will be provided.

Make sure when you begin a practice test that you allow yourself time to finish it in a single sitting. It is important to take the practice tests under conditions that are as similar as possible to the actual testing situation. That means you need to time each section precisely, and that you need to work through each exam from beginning to end.

As you work, follow all instructions precisely. Do not pick up your pencil until you are ready to begin and have started your timer. Have the timer set for the exact number of minutes allowed for each section, and when the timer goes off, stop working immediately. When you take the U.S. Postal Exam, you will be required to leave your test booklet unopened until you are instructed to open it. You will be required to put down your pencil and close your booklet as soon as your time is up. There are no exceptions to these rules, so now is the time to learn to follow them.

When you finish a practice exam, turn to the scoring section near the back of the book and follow the instructions for scoring. It is important that you score each exam as you complete it, so you will be able to track your improvement.

When you are ready to begin this practice exam, get your timer and your pencil ready and turn the page.

Postal Exam 473/473-C
Practice Test Answer Sheet

Tear out or photocopy one two-sided Answer Sheet for each Practice Test. This sheet is similar to the one you will mark at the real exam.

When taking the actual Test 473 or 473-C, you will first fill in the top half of the front side of the Answer Sheet, which asks for information similar to what you provided when applying for the exam. You will mark your answers for Address Checking and Forms Completion on the bottom half of the first side.

On the back side of the Answer Sheet, you will mark your answers for the final two sections of the test: Coding and Memory and Personal Characteristics and Experience Inventory.

For some excellent tips on marking your Answer Sheet, please see **Appendix A: Five Valuable Answer Sheet Marking Strategies** in the back of this book.

Part A: Address Checking

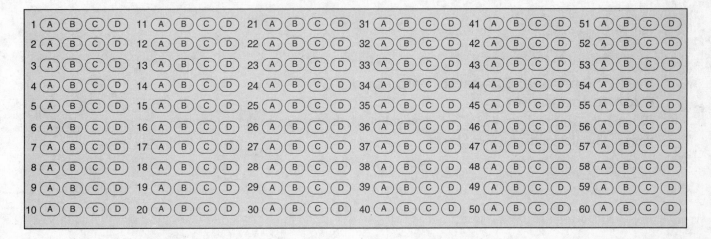

Part B: Forms Completion

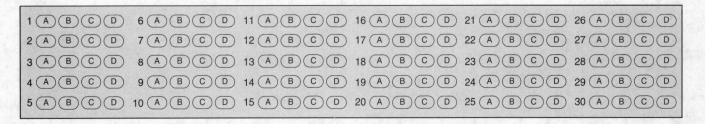

continued on the other side →

KAPLAN

Part C: Coding and Memory

Coding Section		Memory Section	

Coding Section

1 (A) (B) (C) (D)   13 (A) (B) (C) (D)   25 (A) (B) (C) (D)
2 (A) (B) (C) (D)   14 (A) (B) (C) (D)   26 (A) (B) (C) (D)
3 (A) (B) (C) (D)   15 (A) (B) (C) (D)   27 (A) (B) (C) (D)
4 (A) (B) (C) (D)   16 (A) (B) (C) (D)   28 (A) (B) (C) (D)
5 (A) (B) (C) (D)   17 (A) (B) (C) (D)   29 (A) (B) (C) (D)
6 (A) (B) (C) (D)   18 (A) (B) (C) (D)   30 (A) (B) (C) (D)
7 (A) (B) (C) (D)   19 (A) (B) (C) (D)   31 (A) (B) (C) (D)
8 (A) (B) (C) (D)   20 (A) (B) (C) (D)   32 (A) (B) (C) (D)
9 (A) (B) (C) (D)   21 (A) (B) (C) (D)   33 (A) (B) (C) (D)
10 (A) (B) (C) (D)   22 (A) (B) (C) (D)   34 (A) (B) (C) (D)
11 (A) (B) (C) (D)   23 (A) (B) (C) (D)   35 (A) (B) (C) (D)
12 (A) (B) (C) (D)   24 (A) (B) (C) (D)   36 (A) (B) (C) (D)

Memory Section

37 (A) (B) (C) (D)   49 (A) (B) (C) (D)   61 (A) (B) (C) (D)
38 (A) (B) (C) (D)   50 (A) (B) (C) (D)   62 (A) (B) (C) (D)
39 (A) (B) (C) (D)   51 (A) (B) (C) (D)   63 (A) (B) (C) (D)
40 (A) (B) (C) (D)   52 (A) (B) (C) (D)   64 (A) (B) (C) (D)
41 (A) (B) (C) (D)   53 (A) (B) (C) (D)   65 (A) (B) (C) (D)
42 (A) (B) (C) (D)   54 (A) (B) (C) (D)   66 (A) (B) (C) (D)
43 (A) (B) (C) (D)   55 (A) (B) (C) (D)   67 (A) (B) (C) (D)
44 (A) (B) (C) (D)   56 (A) (B) (C) (D)   68 (A) (B) (C) (D)
45 (A) (B) (C) (D)   57 (A) (B) (C) (D)   69 (A) (B) (C) (D)
46 (A) (B) (C) (D)   58 (A) (B) (C) (D)   70 (A) (B) (C) (D)
47 (A) (B) (C) (D)   59 (A) (B) (C) (D) .   71 (A) (B) (C) (D)
48 (A) (B) (C) (D)   60 (A) (B) (C) (D)   72 (A) (B) (C) (D)

Part D: Personal Characteristics and Experience Inventory

[When taking the real Test 473/473-C, you will mark the answers to the 236 questions in this area of the Answer Sheet.]

Part A: Address Checking

Instructions

Part A has 60 questions. You will have 11 minutes to complete this portion of the test. Each item has two side-by-side addresses containing either identical or almost identical information.

You must compare each of the 60 items, decide if they are *exactly* the same or not, and mark the correct answers by blackening the corresponding ovals on your answer sheet. If the two addresses are different, you must decide if there is a difference in only the street address or in only the ZIP code *or* in both the street address *and* the ZIP code.

There are four answer choices, as you can see from the sample below; and the answer sheet has four ovals for each item, representing those four choices. If the two addresses are the same, darken oval A. If there is a difference in the street address only, darken oval B. If there is a difference in the ZIP code only, darken oval C. And if there is a difference in both the street address and the ZIP code, darken oval D.

A. No Errors   B. Address Only   C. ZIP Code Only   D. Both

Set your timer for exactly 11 minutes. Turn the page when you are ready and begin.

Part A: Address Checking

A. No Errors	B. Address Only	C. ZIP Code Only	D. Both

	Correct List		List to Be Checked	
	Address	ZIP Code	Address	ZIP Code
1.	2020 Windmill Dr. Houston, TX	98101	2002 Windmill Dr. Houston, TX	98101
2.	652 Patata St. Athens, GA	25355	652 Patota St. Athens, GA	25535
3.	87 N. Glenoaks Ave. Sylacauga, AL	80754	87 N. Glenoaks Ave. Sylacauga, AL	80754
4.	432 Rigger Road Innsbruck, IL	96504	432 Rigger Road Innsbruck, IL	96504
5.	7063 Meyer Ct. Freerange, UT	65404-9121	7063 Meyer Ct. Freerange, UT	64504-9121
6.	6330 Green Street Birmingham, AL	29257	6330 Greene Street Birmingham, AL	29257
7.	8370 Broad Blvd. Nashville, TN	42581	3870 Broad Blvd. Nashville, TN	42581
8.	65108 Hilly Lane Bakersfield, CA	78673	65108 Hilly Lane Bakersfeld, CA	78673
9.	4434 Walnut Road Youngstown, MI	85868	4434 Walnut Road Youngstown, MI	85868
10.	8340 Holly Circle Parktown, OK	11697	8340 Hilly Circle Parktown, OK	11967
11.	222 Amos Avenue Stillwater, AZ	46768	222 Amos Avenue Stillwater, AZ	46768
12.	26 College View Lane Boise, ID	80707	26 College View Lane Boise, ID	70807
13.	65 Cloverdale St. Tampa, FL	77329	65 Cloverdale St. Tampa, FL	77329
14.	9682 Riva Road Taos, NM	65891	9682 Riva Road Taos, NM	65981
15.	1121 Marby Circle Lighter, MN	35858	1121 Morby Circle Lighter, MN	38558
16.	379 Eaton Place Springton, MA	90502	379 Eaton Place Springston, MA	90502

A. No Errors   B. Address Only   C. ZIP Code Only   D. Both

Correct List		List to Be Checked	
Address	ZIP Code	Address	ZIP Code
17. 55 Dumas Street Sweet Hollow, VA	82025	55 Dumas Street Sweet Hollow, VA	82025
18. 677 Forrest Way Passeo, TX	10783	677 Forrest Way Passeo, TX	10783
19. 2468 Mildred Lane Nanceton, NJ	88592	2468 Mildrid Lane Nanceton, NJ	88952
20. PO Box 6220 Riverdale, WY	47201	PO Box 6220 Riverdale, WY	47021
21. 1991 Island View Rd. Sixshooter, MT	85753	1991 Island View Rd. Sixhooter, MT	85753
22. 59 Goldcrest Way Sierra Cadre, CA	24869	59 Goldcreste Way Sierra Cadre, CA	24869
23. Rural Route 52-B Lake Atlatl, NY	25003	Rural Route 52-B Lake Atlatl, NY	25003
24. 26 Buzzard Peak Ln Childersburg, AL	92478	26 Buzzard Peak Ln Childersburg, AL	92478
25. 1441 Terminal K Seattle, WA	11704	1414 Terminal K Seattle, WA	11704
26. 65 Altura CT Tomboy, PA	29983	65 Altura CT Timboy, PA	29893
27. 1998 Dinwiddy Dr. Charleston, SC	65757	1998 Dinwiddy Dr. Charlestan, SC	56757
28. 100 Kaimaina Circle Honolulu, HI	18753	100 Kaimaina Circle Honolulu, HI	18753
29. 33 W. 63rd Ave. Great Neck, NY	37675	33 W. 63rd Ave. Great Neck, NY	37675
30. 19 Hamview Apt. 6-C Junaluska, NC	79499	19 Hamview Apt. 6-C Junaluska, NC	97499
31. 1667 S. Irving Nicetown, KS	45249	1667 S. Irving Nicetone, KS	45249
32. 239 Jackrabbit Tr. Iberia, OR	81510-2390	239 Jackrabbit Tr. Iburia, OR	81510-2390
33. 1645 Easter LN Smartsville, OH	65752	1645 Easter LN Smartsville, OH	65572
34. 9103 Dwight Dr. Piscatoga, RI	44109	9103 Dwight Dr. Piscataga, RI	41409

A. No Errors	B. Address Only	C. ZIP Code Only	D. Both

Correct List		List to Be Checked	
Address	**ZIP Code**	**Address**	**ZIP Code**
35. 42 Iwanabee Tr. Panama City, FL	25783	42 Iwanabee Tr. Panama City, FL	25783
36. 44 Boothill Place Jacksonville, MS	14321	44 Boothill Place Jacksonville, MS	13421
37. 10407 Liston St. Rome, KY	77283	10407 Litton St. Rome, KY	77382
38. 99 Bottle Brush Way Denver, CO	19492	99 Bottle Brush Way Denver, CO	19492
39. 2015 Rue Roux New Orleans, LA	62268	2015 Rue Roux New Orleans, LA	62628
40. 1201 Da Vinci Portsmith, ME	74627	1201 Da Vinci Portsmouth, ME	74627
41. 55345 S. Bend Rd. Last Chance, IN	38782	55345 W. Bend Rd. Last Chance, IN	38782
42. 34 Parcel Pass Hightown, AR	47821	34 Parcel Pass Hightowne, AR	47821
43. 14092 63rd Ave. Princeton, NJ	93751	14092 63rd Ave. Princeton, NJ	93751
44. 256 W. 19th Apt. G Allentown, VT	72625	256 W. 19th Apt. G Allentown, VT	72265
45. 11 Goodluck LN Las Vegas, NV	38746	11 Goodlick LN Las Vegas, NV	38786
46. 5872 Daley Dr. Seeton, MO	35784	5872 Daley Dr. Seeton, MO	35784
47. 2020 Belair Blvd. Detroit, MI	16672	2020 Belair Blvd. Detroit, MI	16672
48. 16 E. Fork Ave. Lincoln, NB	88201	16 E. Forks Ave. Lincoln, NB	88102
49. 43 Breakneck St. Rodeo, CA	29865	43 Breakneck St. Rodeo, CA	29685
50. 16 Ivy Terrace Charleston, WV	73536	16 Ivy Terrace Charlestan, WV	73536
51. 1100 E. 14th St. Mossville, NH	65243	1100 E. 14th St. Moosville, NH	65243
52. 378 Jaguar Ln Savannah, GA	65728	378 Jagaur Ln Savannah, GA	62578

A. No Errors	B. Address Only	C. ZIP Code Only	D. Both

Correct List		List to Be Checked	
Address	**ZIP Code**	**Address**	**ZIP Code**
53. 14-B Industry Ave. Rehoboth, DE	27878	14-B Industry Ave. Rehoboth, DE	28778
54. 1873 Fir St. Kirkland, WA	65757	1873 Fur St. Kirkland, WA	65757
55. 56 Lamer Lane Akron, OH	25784	56 Lamer Lane Akron, OH	25784
56. 91991 Story Pl Miami, FL	67251	9191 Story Pl Miami, FL	62751
57. 376 Roper Rd. Silver Springs, MD	51208	376 Roper Rd. Silver Springs, MD	51208
58. 80-D Monaco Ave. Pittsburgh, PA	88103	80- Moneco Ave. Pittsburgh, PA	88103
59. 2330 Dawkins Dr. Jackson, IA	20784	2330 Dawkins Dr. Jackson, IA	20784
60. 8330 Simmons Way Wilkinson, MT	43071	8330 Simmons Way Wilkinson, MT	40371

This is the end of Part A: Address Checking Section, Practice Test 1.

Part B: Forms Completion

Part B consists of 30 questions that test your ability to identify the information needed to correctly complete various U.S. Postal Service forms. You will be shown 5 different forms similar to real-life USPS forms. Each form will be followed by 6 questions.

Set your timer for exactly 15 minutes. Turn the page and begin when you are ready.

Part B: Forms Completion

Domestic Return Receipt

SENDER: COMPLETE THIS SECTION	COMPLETE THIS SECTION UPON DELIVERY
■ Complete items 1, 2, and 3. Also complete item 4 if Restricted Delivery is desired. ■ Print your name and address on the reverse so that we can return the card to you. ■ Attach this card to the back of the mailpiece, or on the front if space permits.	A. Signature X ☐ Agent ☐ Addressee B. Received by (Printed Name) C. Date of Delivery
1. Article Addressed to:	D. Is delivery address different from item 1? ☐ Yes If YES, enter delivery address below: ☐ No
	3. Service Type ☐ Certified Mail ☐ Express Mail ☐ Registered ☐ Return Receipt for Merchandise ☐ Insured Mail
	4. Restricted Delivery? (Extra Fee) ☐ Yes
2. Article Number (Transfer from service label)	

Part B: Forms Completion

1. Which of these would be a correct entry for Box C?
   A. Ned Racine
   B. 351 West 19th Street
   C. 4:00 p.m.
   D. 06/12/07

2. What should be printed on the reverse of this form?
   A. The service type
   B. The addressee's name and address
   C. The sender's name and address
   D. The article number

3. Where would a check mark be appropriate?
   A. Box A
   B. Box D
   C. Box 3
   D. All of the above

4. Lisa Bartlett received the package. Where should her name be printed?
   A. Box A
   B. Box B
   C. Box C
   D. Box D

5. The Article Number is 32-6813-05. Where would you indicate this?
   A. Box 2
   B. Box 3
   C. Box 4
   D. None of these

6. If Restricted Delivery is desired, where would this be indicated?
   A. Box 1
   B. Box 2
   C. Box 3
   D. Box 4

Part B: Forms Completion

Express Mail Mailing Label

1a. Date Accepted Mo. Day Year	**1b.** Postage $
2a. Time Accepted ☐ AM ☐ PM	**2b.** Return Receipt Fee $

3a. Flat Rate ☐ or Weight lbs. ozs.	**3b.** COD Fee $	**3c.** Insurance Fee $

4a. PO ZIP Code	**4b.** Total Postage & Fees $

5. FROM: (PLEASE PRINT ADDRESS) PHONE ( )＿＿＿＿＿＿＿＿	**6.** TO: (PLEASE PRINT ADDRESS) PHONE ( )＿＿＿＿＿＿＿＿

Part B: Forms Completion

7. In which of these would $15.74 be an acceptable entry?
   A. Either Box 1a or 1b
   B. Either Box 2a or 2b
   C. Either Box 1b or 4b
   D. Either Box 5 or 6

8. Which boxes might include the ZIP Code 62115?
   A. Box 4a
   B. Box 5
   C. Box 6
   D. All of the above

9. How should it be indicated that the item is being sent Flat Rate?
   A. Make a note in Box 1a
   B. Check "Flat Rate" in Box 2a
   C. Check "Flat Rate" in Box 3a
   D. None of the above

10. Which of these would best be entered in Box 3a?
   A. 3 lbs., 5 ozs.
   B. Dr. Martin Silkowski
   C. $14.87
   D. 10:23

11. The Return Receipt Fee is $1.50. Where would this amount be entered?
   A. Box 1a
   B. Box 2b
   C. Box 3b
   D. Box 6

12. Which would be an appropriate entry for Box 1a?
   A. 9 lbs., 4 ozs.
   B. 04/28/2006
   C. 91030
   D. Ms. Caroline Murray

Part B: Forms Completion

Authorization to Hold Mail

Postmaster, **Please hold mail for:**	
1a. Name(s)	**Note:** We can hold your mail for a minimum of **3 days**, but not for more than **30 days**.
2a. Address *(Number, street, apt./suite no., city, state, ZIP + 4)*	**2b.** I will pick up all accumulated mail when I return and understand that mail delivery will not resume until I do so. *Customer Signature* _____
3. Beginning Date	
For Post Office Use Only	
4a. Date Received	**4b.** PO ZIP Code
5a. Clerk	**5b.** Bin Number
6a. Carrier	**6b.** Route Number
Resumption of Mail Delivery	
☐ **7.** Accumulated mail has been picked up.	**8.** Resume Delivery of Mail *(Date)*
	9. By

Part B: Forms Completion

13. Which would be an appropriate entry for Box 2a?
   A. 42 Lone Wolf Lane, Pico, GA 30012
   B. September 12, 2006
   C. 53
   D. Grace Wherry

14. Which would be an appropriate entry for Box 5b?
   A. 42 Lone Wolf Lane, Pico, GA 30012
   B. September 12, 2006
   C. 53
   D. Grace Wherry

15. Which box will indicate to the carrier when mail delivery can be resumed?
   A. Box 3
   B. Box 4a
   C. Box 6b
   D. Box 8

16. Where should the carrier's route number be entered?
   A. Box 6a
   B. Box 6b
   C. Box 7
   D. Box 9

17. In which of these should a name be entered?
   A. Box 1a
   B. Boxes 5a and 6a
   C. Box 9
   D. All of the above

18. What would indicate that the customer's accumulated mail has been picked up?
   A. A signature in Box 2b
   B. A date in Box 4a
   C. A check mark in Box 7
   D. All of the above

Part B: Forms Completion

Application for Post Office Box or Caller Service – Part 1

Customer: Complete items 1, 3-6

1. Name(s) to Which Box Number(s) Is (are) Assigned	2. Box or Caller Numbers _____ through _____
3. Name of Person Applying, Title *(if representing an organization)*, and Name of Organization *(if Different From Item 1)*	4a. Will This Box Be Used for: ☐ Personal Use ☐ Business Use *(Optional)*
5. Address *(Number, street, apt. no., city, state, and ZIP Code™)*. When address changes, cross out address here and put new address on back.	4b. Email Address *(Optional)*
	6. Telephone Number *(Include area code)*

7. Date Application Received	8. Box Size Needed	9. ID and Physical Address Verified by *(Initials)*	10. Dates of Service _____ through _____

Part B: Forms Completion

19. Where should the size of the box to be rented be entered?
- A. Box 2
- B. Box 4a
- C. Box 6
- D. Box 8

20. Where would a check mark for "Business Use" be appropriately placed?
- A. In Box 2
- B. In Box 4a
- C. In either Box 4a or Box 4b
- D. In either Box 4a or Box 8

21. Which box or boxes ask for optional information?
- A. Box 4a
- B. Boxes 1 and 2
- C. Boxes 4a and 4b
- D. Box 10

22. In which of these boxes could a full date such as 04/02/06 be entered?
- A. Box 2
- B. Box 3
- C. Box 7
- D. Boxes 7 and 10

23. Which is a correct entry for Box 9?
- A. KH
- B. Dr. Simon Nellis
- C. 215-405-7736
- D. Personal Use

24. What goes into Box 3?
- A. The name of the person applying, if different from Box 1
- B. The address of the person applying, if different from Box 1
- C. The box or caller numbers
- D. The date the application was received

Part B: Forms Completion

Global Direct Notification of Mailing

A. General

1. Mailer's Name	2. Mailer's Address *(No., street, ste. no., city, state, ZIP + 4)*
3. Contact Person	
4a. Telephone No. *(Include area code)*	
4b. Fax No. *(Include area code)*	

5. Destination Country	6. Date Notified	7. Global Direct Customer ID No.

B. Mailing Information

8. Mailing Date	9. Estimated Total Mailing Weight	10. Container Quantity Trays _____ Pallets _____	11. Acceptance Location ☐ Plant-Verification Drop Shipment Location: ☐ Global Direct Acceptance Location:

12. Return Address *(See PS Form 3681 including Global Direct Customer Identification Number.)* Check the appropriate box: ☐ I will use my own in-country return address ☐ I will use the following USPS-provided in-country return address:	13. I am requesting the return of "Undeliverable-As-Addressed" items to the USPS in-country return address. I would like these items sent to the following US address *(No., street, ste. no, city, state, ZIP + 4)*:

NOTE: General correspondence and other items may occasionally be sent to this address by customers in the destination country. I agree to pay the USPS for the return of such items to my designated US address. For rate information, see the *IMM* and USPS publications on Global Direct Service.

C. Comments

Part B: Forms Completion

25. The mailing date would be documented in which box?
  A. Box 6
  B. Box 8
  C. Box 9
  D. Box 11

26. Where would a FAX number be entered?
  A. Box 1
  B. Box 2
  C. Box 4a
  D. Box 4b

27. Where would the number of pallets, if any, be entered?
  A. Box 7
  B. Box 10
  C. Box 10 or Box 11
  D. Under "C. Comments"

28. Which of these could be a correct entry for either Box 1 or Box 3?
  A. Philippe Verde
  B. Thailand
  C. October 21, 2006
  D. 34 lbs., 13 ozs.

29. The customer's destination country is Senegal. Where should this information be entered?
  A. Box 3
  B. Box 6
  C. Box 7
  D. None of the above

30. The address for the "Undeliverable-As-Addressed" items would be entered into which Box?
  A. Box 2
  B. Box 11
  C. Box 13
  D. Under "C. Comments"

Part C: Coding and Memory

Overview

In Part C you will need to work quickly and accurately, using one Coding Guide to answer questions in two separate sections, the Coding Section and the Memory Section.

Prior to the scored segments of both the Coding Section and the Memory Section, there are practice segments. This test will follow the same format.

The Coding Guide that is used throughout Part C consists of four delivery routes. Three of the routes have two or three address ranges associated with them, and the last route covers any address not within the other three routes.

Each question (item) in both the Coding Section and the Memory Section consists of an address. Your job is to determine which of the four routes a given address belongs to and to mark your answer sheet accordingly.

In the Coding Section you may use the Coding Guide to determine the correct route for each address. In the Memory Section you will see exactly the same type of questions that are in the Coding Section, but you will no longer be able to look at the Coding Guide. Rather, you must determine which of the four routes an address belongs to, using only your memory of the Coding Guide.

The scored portion of the Coding Section has 36 questions, and you have six minutes to answer them. Prior to the scored portion, you will have two opportunities to practice using the Coding Guide.

The scored portion of the Memory Section also has 36 questions and 7 minutes to answer them. It also provides you with two opportunities to study and memorize the Coding Guide, as well as a chance to practice answering questions without using the Coding Guide.

Part C: Coding Section

Part 1: Sample Questions

Instructions   Answering the questions on the following pages will familiarize you with the format and timing of the questions in Part C: Coding Section. You will have 3½ minutes to answer 12 questions, using the Coding Guide displayed opposite the questions.

Mark your answers in the sample ovals and check your answers using the correct answers shown at the bottom of the same page.

Set your timer for 3½ minutes and turn the page when you are ready to begin.

Part C: Coding Section

Coding Guide

Address Range	Delivery Route
1–99 Sunrise Place 11–201 W 57th Street 50–150 Ambrose Way	A
200–400 Hillhurst Drive 202–301 W 57th Street	B
60000–62000 National Blvd. 300–310 Harvard Lane 16–26 Rural Route 2	C
Any mail that is not found in one of the above address ranges	D

Part C: Coding Section

Exercise 1: Sample Questions

	Address	Delivery Route			
1.	199 W 57th Street	Ⓐ	Ⓑ	Ⓒ	Ⓓ
2.	61050 National Blvd.	Ⓐ	Ⓑ	Ⓒ	Ⓓ
3.	208 W 57th Street	Ⓐ	Ⓑ	Ⓒ	Ⓓ
4.	98 Sunrose Place	Ⓐ	Ⓑ	Ⓒ	Ⓓ
5.	13 W 57th Street	Ⓐ	Ⓑ	Ⓒ	Ⓓ
6.	309 Hillhurst Drive	Ⓐ	Ⓑ	Ⓒ	Ⓓ
7.	287 W 57th Street	Ⓐ	Ⓑ	Ⓒ	Ⓓ
8.	301 Harvard Lane	Ⓐ	Ⓑ	Ⓒ	Ⓓ
9.	16 Rural Route 3	Ⓐ	Ⓑ	Ⓒ	Ⓓ
10.	51 Ambrose Way	Ⓐ	Ⓑ	Ⓒ	Ⓓ
11.	60009 National Blvd.	Ⓐ	Ⓑ	Ⓒ	Ⓓ
12.	97 Sunrise Place	Ⓐ	Ⓑ	Ⓒ	Ⓓ

Answers

1. A
2. C
3. B
4. D
5. A
6. B
7. B
8. C
9. D
10. A
11. C
12. A

KAPLAN

Part C: Coding Section

Coding Practice Test 1

Instructions   This section follows the format of Postal Exam 473. There are 36 questions, and you will have 6 minutes to answer them. Each page of questions is displayed opposite the Coding Guide, which you may use to answer the questions.

You will score this section and use it to help determine your score on this practice test. Mark your answers on your Practice Test 1 Answer Sheet in the Coding Section of Part C.

Set your timer for 6 minutes and turn the page when you are ready to begin.

Coding Section: Practice Test 1

Coding Guide

Address Range	Delivery Route
1–99 Sunrise Place 11–201 W 57th Street 50–150 Ambrose Way	A
200–400 Hillhurst Drive 202–301 W 57th Street	B
60000–62000 National Blvd. 300–310 Harvard Lane 16–26 Rural Route 2	C
Any mail that is not found in one of the above address ranges	D

Coding Section: Practice Test 1
Questions

	Address	Delivery Route
1.	301 Harvard Lane	Ⓐ Ⓑ Ⓒ Ⓓ
2.	62001 National Blvd.	Ⓐ Ⓑ Ⓒ Ⓓ
3.	121 W 57th Street	Ⓐ Ⓑ Ⓒ Ⓓ
4.	59 Ambrose Way	Ⓐ Ⓑ Ⓒ Ⓓ
5.	17 Rural Route 3	Ⓐ Ⓑ Ⓒ Ⓓ
6.	300 Hillhurst Drive	Ⓐ Ⓑ Ⓒ Ⓓ
7.	60100 National Blvd.	Ⓐ Ⓑ Ⓒ Ⓓ
8.	17 Rural Route 2	Ⓐ Ⓑ Ⓒ Ⓓ
9.	78 Sunrise Place	Ⓐ Ⓑ Ⓒ Ⓓ
10.	149 Ambrose Way	Ⓐ Ⓑ Ⓒ Ⓓ
11.	212 W 57th Street	Ⓐ Ⓑ Ⓒ Ⓓ
12.	308 Harvard Drive	Ⓐ Ⓑ Ⓒ Ⓓ
13.	61060 National Blvd.	Ⓐ Ⓑ Ⓒ Ⓓ
14.	201 Hillhurst Drive	Ⓐ Ⓑ Ⓒ Ⓓ
15.	300 W 57th Street	Ⓐ Ⓑ Ⓒ Ⓓ
16.	25 Rural Route 2	Ⓐ Ⓑ Ⓒ Ⓓ
17.	62010 National Blvd.	Ⓐ Ⓑ Ⓒ Ⓓ
18.	10 Sunrise Place	Ⓐ Ⓑ Ⓒ Ⓓ
19.	284 W 57th Street	Ⓐ Ⓑ Ⓒ Ⓓ
20.	309 Harvard Lane	Ⓐ Ⓑ Ⓒ Ⓓ
21.	60009 National Blvd.	Ⓐ Ⓑ Ⓒ Ⓓ

Coding Guide	
Address Range	**Delivery Route**
1–99 Sunrise Place 11–201 W 57th Street 50–150 Ambrose Way	A
200–400 Hillhurst Drive 202–301 W 57th Street	B
60000–62000 National Blvd. 30–310 Harvard Lane 16–26 Rural Route 2	C
Any mail that is not found in one of the above address ranges	D

22.	55 Ambrose Way	Ⓐ Ⓑ Ⓒ Ⓓ
23.	200 Hillhurst Lane	Ⓐ Ⓑ Ⓒ Ⓓ
24.	55 Sunrise Place	Ⓐ Ⓑ Ⓒ Ⓓ
25.	278 W 57th Street	Ⓐ Ⓑ Ⓒ Ⓓ
26.	205 Hillhurst Drive	Ⓐ Ⓑ Ⓒ Ⓓ
27.	61135 National Blvd.	Ⓐ Ⓑ Ⓒ Ⓓ
28.	149 Ambrose Place	Ⓐ Ⓑ Ⓒ Ⓓ
29.	110 W 57th Street	Ⓐ Ⓑ Ⓒ Ⓓ
30.	101 Ambrose Way	Ⓐ Ⓑ Ⓒ Ⓓ
31.	308 Harvard Lane	Ⓐ Ⓑ Ⓒ Ⓓ
32.	299 W 57th Street	Ⓐ Ⓑ Ⓒ Ⓓ
33.	60505 National Blvd.	Ⓐ Ⓑ Ⓒ Ⓓ
34.	200 W 57th Street	Ⓐ Ⓑ Ⓒ Ⓓ
35.	60505 National Blvd.	Ⓐ Ⓑ Ⓒ Ⓓ
36.	147 Ambrose Place	Ⓐ Ⓑ Ⓒ Ⓓ

This is the end of Part C: Coding Section, Practice Test 1.

Part C: Memory Section

Overview

There are four divisions in Part C: Memory Section. They are

1. a 3-minute period for studying the Coding Guide;
2. a 90-second nonscored practice, in which you answer 8 questions without using the Coding Guide;
3. a 5-minute period for studying the Coding Guide; and
4. a scored test, consisting of 36 questions, timed for 7 minutes.

During the two study periods there are no questions to answer; you are memorizing the Coding Guide. Section 2 is a timed practice test, with eight questions to answer in 90 seconds, and a sample answer sheet. Section 4 is the actual test. Use the Practice Test 1 answer sheet to mark your answers. They will be scored.

Memory Section: Part 1

Instructions

Part 1 of the Memory Section is a study period. Use it to memorize the Coding Guide. There are no questions to answer during the 3-minute study period.

Set your timer for 3 minutes, and when you are ready to begin, turn the page.

Memory Section: Part 1

Coding Guide	
Address Range	**Delivery Route**
1–99 Sunrise Place 11–201 W 57th Street 50–150 Ambrose Way	A
200–400 Hillhurst Drive 202–301 W 57th Street	B
60000–62000 National Blvd. 300–310 Harvard Lane 16–26 Rural Route 2	C
Any mail that is not found in one of the above address ranges	D

Memory Section: Part 2

Instructions

In Part 2 of the Memory Section, you will practice answering questions using your memory of the Coding Guide (see p. 73), which will not be shown. This is only a practice exercise; it will not be scored.

Following the eight questions is a sample answer sheet that you will use to mark your answers. At the bottom of the page is the answer key for the sample questions.

Set your timer for 90 seconds; when you are ready, you may begin.

]]][MONTROSE REGIONAL
LIBRARY DISTRICT

www.montroselibrary.org • 970-249-9656

Customer ID: ***********4780

Items that you checked out

Title: Kaplan postal exam 473/473-C.
ID: 11100040256532
Due: Friday, December 3, 2021

Total items: 1
Account balance: $0.00
11/19/2021 12:36 PM
Checked out: 1
Overdue: 0
Hold requests: 0
Ready for pickup: 0

Renew by phone: 249-9656

Memory Section: Part 2

	Address	Delivery Route			
1.	61000 National Blvd.	Ⓐ	Ⓑ	Ⓒ	Ⓓ
2.	311 Harvard Lane	Ⓐ	Ⓑ	Ⓒ	Ⓓ
3.	95 Sunrise Place	Ⓐ	Ⓑ	Ⓒ	Ⓓ
4.	149 Ambrose Way	Ⓐ	Ⓑ	Ⓒ	Ⓓ
5.	244 W 57th Street	Ⓐ	Ⓑ	Ⓒ	Ⓓ
6.	24 Rural Route 2	Ⓐ	Ⓑ	Ⓒ	Ⓓ
7.	269 Hillhurst Drive	Ⓐ	Ⓑ	Ⓒ	Ⓓ
8.	178 W 57th Street	Ⓐ	Ⓑ	Ⓒ	Ⓓ

Answers

1. C
2. D
3. A
4. A
5. B
6. C
7. B
8. A

Memory Section: Part 3

Instructions

Part 3 of the Memory Section is a 5-minute study period. This is your final preparation period for the scored Memory test. Use it to finish memorizing the Coding Guide. As in Part 1 of this section, there are no questions to answer. Do not make marks of any kind during this study period.

Set your timer for 5 minutes, and when you are ready, turn the page and begin.

Memory Section: Part 3

Coding Guide	
Address Range	**Delivery Route**
1–99 Sunrise Place 11–201 W 57th Street 50–150 Ambrose Way	A
200–400 Hillhurst Drive 202–301 W 57th Street	B
60000–62000 National Blvd. 300–310 Harvard Lane 16–26 Rural Route 2	C
Any mail that is not found in one of the above address ranges	D

Memory Section: Part 4

Instructions

Part 4 of the Memory Section is the scored Memory test. You will have 7 minutes to answer the 36 questions, without using the Coding Guide. You must answer the questions from memory.

Mark your answers to these 36 questions on the Practice Test 1 Answer Sheet, using lines 37–72 of Part C: Coding and Memory. When you have finished, it is time to score the exam.

Set your timer for 7 minutes, and when you are ready, begin.

Memory Section: Practice Test 1

Questions

	Address	Delivery Route			
37.	311 Hillhurst Drive	(A)	(B)	(C)	(D)
38.	116 Ambrose Way	(A)	(B)	(C)	(D)
39.	111 W 57th Street	(A)	(B)	(C)	(D)
40.	309 Harvard Lane	(A)	(B)	(C)	(D)
41.	301 W 57th Street	(A)	(B)	(C)	(D)
42.	99 Sunset Place	(A)	(B)	(C)	(D)
43.	20 Rural Route 2	(A)	(B)	(C)	(D)
44.	60002 National Blvd.	(A)	(B)	(C)	(D)
45.	60 Ambrose Way	(A)	(B)	(C)	(D)
46.	380 Hillhurst Drive	(A)	(B)	(C)	(D)
47.	400 Hillhurst Drive	(A)	(B)	(C)	(D)
48.	201 W 57th Street	(A)	(B)	(C)	(D)
49.	401 W 57th Street	(A)	(B)	(C)	(D)
50.	300 Harvard Lane	(A)	(B)	(C)	(D)
51.	61010 National Blvd.	(A)	(B)	(C)	(D)
52.	100 Ambrose Way	(A)	(B)	(C)	(D)
53.	11 Sunrise Place	(A)	(B)	(C)	(D)
54.	300 W 57th Street	(A)	(B)	(C)	(D)
55.	16 Rural Route 2	(A)	(B)	(C)	(D)
56.	255 W 57th Street	(A)	(B)	(C)	(D)

57.	65 Sunrise Place	Ⓐ Ⓑ Ⓒ Ⓓ
58.	21 W 57th Street	Ⓐ Ⓑ Ⓒ Ⓓ
59.	6200 National Blvd.	Ⓐ Ⓑ Ⓒ Ⓓ
60.	125 Ambrose Way	Ⓐ Ⓑ Ⓒ Ⓓ
61.	307 Harvard Lane	Ⓐ Ⓑ Ⓒ Ⓓ
62.	250 Hillhurst Drive	Ⓐ Ⓑ Ⓒ Ⓓ
63.	26 Rural Route 2	Ⓐ Ⓑ Ⓒ Ⓓ
64.	61616 National Blvd.	Ⓐ Ⓑ Ⓒ Ⓓ
65.	303 Harvard Lane	Ⓐ Ⓑ Ⓒ Ⓓ
66.	399 Hillhurst Drive	Ⓐ Ⓑ Ⓒ Ⓓ
67.	12 W 57th Street	Ⓐ Ⓑ Ⓒ Ⓓ
68.	267 W 57th Street	Ⓐ Ⓑ Ⓒ Ⓓ
69.	167 W 57th Street	Ⓐ Ⓑ Ⓒ Ⓓ
70.	309 Hillhurst Drive	Ⓐ Ⓑ Ⓒ Ⓓ
71.	51 Ambrose Way	Ⓐ Ⓑ Ⓒ Ⓓ
72.	6 Rural Route 2	Ⓐ Ⓑ Ⓒ Ⓓ

This is the end of Part C: Coding Section, Practice Test 1.

Part D: Personal Characteristics and Experience Inventory

As explained earlier, it is not possible to prepare for or practice the 236 job-related characteristics and experience questions in Part D. Therefore, no test items are included in this practice exam. For examples, please see Chapters 2 and 6.

Remember, there are no right or wrong answers in this section of Postal Test 473/473-C. Moreover, the USPS does not reveal how it evaluates the highly personal responses to Part D, nor how it weighs this part.

Feel confident that if you select the one response for each statement/question that best reflects your own personality, experience, and work ethics, you will be honestly representing yourself.

ANSWER KEY FOR PRACTICE TEST 1

Part A: Address Checking

1. B		21. B		41. B	
2. D		22. B		42. B	
3. A		23. A		43. A	
4. A		24. A		44. C	
5. C		25. B		45. D	
6. B		26. D		46. A	
7. B		27. D		47. A	
8. B		28. A		48. D	
9. A		29. A		49. C	
10. D		30. C		50. B	
11. A		31. B		51. B	
12. C		32. B		52. D	
13. A		33. C		53. C	
14. C		34. D		54. B	
15. D		35. A		55. A	
16. B		36. C		56. D	
17. A		37. D		57. A	
18. A		38. A		58. B	
19. D		39. C		59. A	
20. C		40. B		60. C	

KAPLAN

Part B: Forms Completion

1.	D	11.	B	21.	C
2.	C	12.	B	22.	C
3.	D	13.	A	23.	A
4.	B	14.	C	24.	A
5.	A	15.	D	25.	B
6.	D	16.	B	26.	D
7.	C	17.	D	27.	B
8.	D	18.	C	28.	A
9.	C	19.	D	29.	D
10.	A	20.	B	30.	C

Part C: Coding and Memory

1.	C	25.	B	49.	D
2.	D	26.	B	50.	C
3.	A	27.	C	51.	C
4.	A	28.	D	52.	A
5.	D	29.	A	53.	A
6.	B	30.	A	54.	B
7.	C	31.	C	55.	C
8.	C	32.	B	56.	B
9.	A	33.	C	57.	A
10.	A	34.	A	58.	A
11.	B	35.	C	59.	D
12.	D	36.	A	60.	A
13.	C	37.	B	61.	C
14.	B	38.	A	62.	B
15.	B	39.	A	63.	C
16.	C	40.	C	64.	C
17.	D	41.	B	65.	C
18.	A	42.	D	66.	B
19.	B	43.	C	67.	A
20.	C	44.	C	68.	B
21.	C	45.	A	69.	A
22.	A	46.	B	70.	B
23.	D	47.	B	71.	A
24.	A	48.	A	72.	D

Postal Exam 473/473-C
Practice Test Answer Sheet

Tear out or photocopy one two-sided Answer Sheet for each Practice Test. This sheet is similar to the one you will mark at the real exam.

When taking the actual Test 473 or 473-C, you will first fill in the top half of the front side of the Answer Sheet, which asks for information similar to what you provided when applying for the exam. You will mark your answers for Address Checking and Forms Completion on the bottom half of the first side.

On the back side of the Answer Sheet, you will mark your answers for the final two sections of the test: Coding and Memory and Personal Characteristics and Experience Inventory.

For some excellent tips on marking your Answer Sheet, please see **Appendix A: Five Valuable Answer Sheet Marking Strategies.**

Part A: Address Checking

1 Ⓐ Ⓑ Ⓒ Ⓓ	11 Ⓐ Ⓑ Ⓒ Ⓓ	21 Ⓐ Ⓑ Ⓒ Ⓓ	31 Ⓐ Ⓑ Ⓒ Ⓓ	41 Ⓐ Ⓑ Ⓒ Ⓓ	51 Ⓐ Ⓑ Ⓒ Ⓓ
2 Ⓐ Ⓑ Ⓒ Ⓓ	12 Ⓐ Ⓑ Ⓒ Ⓓ	22 Ⓐ Ⓑ Ⓒ Ⓓ	32 Ⓐ Ⓑ Ⓒ Ⓓ	42 Ⓐ Ⓑ Ⓒ Ⓓ	52 Ⓐ Ⓑ Ⓒ Ⓓ
3 Ⓐ Ⓑ Ⓒ Ⓓ	13 Ⓐ Ⓑ Ⓒ Ⓓ	23 Ⓐ Ⓑ Ⓒ Ⓓ	33 Ⓐ Ⓑ Ⓒ Ⓓ	43 Ⓐ Ⓑ Ⓒ Ⓓ	53 Ⓐ Ⓑ Ⓒ Ⓓ
4 Ⓐ Ⓑ Ⓒ Ⓓ	14 Ⓐ Ⓑ Ⓒ Ⓓ	24 Ⓐ Ⓑ Ⓒ Ⓓ	34 Ⓐ Ⓑ Ⓒ Ⓓ	44 Ⓐ Ⓑ Ⓒ Ⓓ	54 Ⓐ Ⓑ Ⓒ Ⓓ
5 Ⓐ Ⓑ Ⓒ Ⓓ	15 Ⓐ Ⓑ Ⓒ Ⓓ	25 Ⓐ Ⓑ Ⓒ Ⓓ	35 Ⓐ Ⓑ Ⓒ Ⓓ	45 Ⓐ Ⓑ Ⓒ Ⓓ	55 Ⓐ Ⓑ Ⓒ Ⓓ
6 Ⓐ Ⓑ Ⓒ Ⓓ	16 Ⓐ Ⓑ Ⓒ Ⓓ	26 Ⓐ Ⓑ Ⓒ Ⓓ	36 Ⓐ Ⓑ Ⓒ Ⓓ	46 Ⓐ Ⓑ Ⓒ Ⓓ	56 Ⓐ Ⓑ Ⓒ Ⓓ
7 Ⓐ Ⓑ Ⓒ Ⓓ	17 Ⓐ Ⓑ Ⓒ Ⓓ	27 Ⓐ Ⓑ Ⓒ Ⓓ	37 Ⓐ Ⓑ Ⓒ Ⓓ	47 Ⓐ Ⓑ Ⓒ Ⓓ	57 Ⓐ Ⓑ Ⓒ Ⓓ
8 Ⓐ Ⓑ Ⓒ Ⓓ	18 Ⓐ Ⓑ Ⓒ Ⓓ	28 Ⓐ Ⓑ Ⓒ Ⓓ	38 Ⓐ Ⓑ Ⓒ Ⓓ	48 Ⓐ Ⓑ Ⓒ Ⓓ	58 Ⓐ Ⓑ Ⓒ Ⓓ
9 Ⓐ Ⓑ Ⓒ Ⓓ	19 Ⓐ Ⓑ Ⓒ Ⓓ	29 Ⓐ Ⓑ Ⓒ Ⓓ	39 Ⓐ Ⓑ Ⓒ Ⓓ	49 Ⓐ Ⓑ Ⓒ Ⓓ	59 Ⓐ Ⓑ Ⓒ Ⓓ
10 Ⓐ Ⓑ Ⓒ Ⓓ	20 Ⓐ Ⓑ Ⓒ Ⓓ	30 Ⓐ Ⓑ Ⓒ Ⓓ	40 Ⓐ Ⓑ Ⓒ Ⓓ	50 Ⓐ Ⓑ Ⓒ Ⓓ	60 Ⓐ Ⓑ Ⓒ Ⓓ

Part B: Forms Completion

1 Ⓐ Ⓑ Ⓒ Ⓓ	6 Ⓐ Ⓑ Ⓒ Ⓓ	11 Ⓐ Ⓑ Ⓒ Ⓓ	16 Ⓐ Ⓑ Ⓒ Ⓓ	21 Ⓐ Ⓑ Ⓒ Ⓓ	26 Ⓐ Ⓑ Ⓒ Ⓓ
2 Ⓐ Ⓑ Ⓒ Ⓓ	7 Ⓐ Ⓑ Ⓒ Ⓓ	12 Ⓐ Ⓑ Ⓒ Ⓓ	17 Ⓐ Ⓑ Ⓒ Ⓓ	22 Ⓐ Ⓑ Ⓒ Ⓓ	27 Ⓐ Ⓑ Ⓒ Ⓓ
3 Ⓐ Ⓑ Ⓒ Ⓓ	8 Ⓐ Ⓑ Ⓒ Ⓓ	13 Ⓐ Ⓑ Ⓒ Ⓓ	18 Ⓐ Ⓑ Ⓒ Ⓓ	23 Ⓐ Ⓑ Ⓒ Ⓓ	28 Ⓐ Ⓑ Ⓒ Ⓓ
4 Ⓐ Ⓑ Ⓒ Ⓓ	9 Ⓐ Ⓑ Ⓒ Ⓓ	14 Ⓐ Ⓑ Ⓒ Ⓓ	19 Ⓐ Ⓑ Ⓒ Ⓓ	24 Ⓐ Ⓑ Ⓒ Ⓓ	29 Ⓐ Ⓑ Ⓒ Ⓓ
5 Ⓐ Ⓑ Ⓒ Ⓓ	10 Ⓐ Ⓑ Ⓒ Ⓓ	15 Ⓐ Ⓑ Ⓒ Ⓓ	20 Ⓐ Ⓑ Ⓒ Ⓓ	25 Ⓐ Ⓑ Ⓒ Ⓓ	30 Ⓐ Ⓑ Ⓒ Ⓓ

continued on the other side →

KAPLAN

Part C: Coding and Memory

	Coding Section					Memory Section	

Coding Section

1 (A) (B) (C) (D) 13 (A) (B) (C) (D) 25 (A) (B) (C) (D)
2 (A) (B) (C) (D) 14 (A) (B) (C) (D) 26 (A) (B) (C) (D)
3 (A) (B) (C) (D) 15 (A) (B) (C) (D) 27 (A) (B) (C) (D)
4 (A) (B) (C) (D) 16 (A) (B) (C) (D) 28 (A) (B) (C) (D)
5 (A) (B) (C) (D) 17 (A) (B) (C) (D) 29 (A) (B) (C) (D)
6 (A) (B) (C) (D) 18 (A) (B) (C) (D) 30 (A) (B) (C) (D)
7 (A) (B) (C) (D) 19 (A) (B) (C) (D) 31 (A) (B) (C) (D)
8 (A) (B) (C) (D) 20 (A) (B) (C) (D) 32 (A) (B) (C) (D)
9 (A) (B) (C) (D) 21 (A) (B) (C) (D) 33 (A) (B) (C) (D)
10 (A) (B) (C) (D) 22 (A) (B) (C) (D) 34 (A) (B) (C) (D)
11 (A) (B) (C) (D) 23 (A) (B) (C) (D) 35 (A) (B) (C) (D)
12 (A) (B) (C) (D) 24 (A) (B) (C) (D) 36 (A) (B) (C) (D)

Memory Section

37 (A) (B) (C) (D) 49 (A) (B) (C) (D) 61 (A) (B) (C) (D)
38 (A) (B) (C) (D) 50 (A) (B) (C) (D) 62 (A) (B) (C) (D)
39 (A) (B) (C) (D) 51 (A) (B) (C) (D) 63 (A) (B) (C) (D)
40 (A) (B) (C) (D) 52 (A) (B) (C) (D) 64 (A) (B) (C) (D)
41 (A) (B) (C) (D) 53 (A) (B) (C) (D) 65 (A) (B) (C) (D)
42 (A) (B) (C) (D) 54 (A) (B) (C) (D) 66 (A) (B) (C) (D)
43 (A) (B) (C) (D) 55 (A) (B) (C) (D) 67 (A) (B) (C) (D)
44 (A) (B) (C) (D) 56 (A) (B) (C) (D) 68 (A) (B) (C) (D)
45 (A) (B) (C) (D) 57 (A) (B) (C) (D) 69 (A) (B) (C) (D)
46 (A) (B) (C) (D) 58 (A) (B) (C) (D) 70 (A) (B) (C) (D)
47 (A) (B) (C) (D) 59 (A) (B) (C) (D) 71 (A) (B) (C) (D)
48 (A) (B) (C) (D) 60 (A) (B) (C) (D) 72 (A) (B) (C) (D)

Part D: Personal Characteristics and Experience Inventory

[When taking the real Test 473/473-C, you will mark the answers to the 236 questions in this area of the Answer Sheet.]

Part A: Address Checking

Instructions

Part A has 60 questions. You will have 11 minutes to complete this portion of the test. Each item (question) has two side-by-side addresses containing either identical or almost identical information.

    You must compare each of the 60 items, decide if they are exactly the same or not, and mark the correct answers by blackening the corresponding ovals on your answer sheet. If the two addresses are different, you must decide if there is a difference in only the street address *or* in only the ZIP code *or* in both the street address *and* the ZIP code.

    There are four answer choices, as you can see from the sample below; and the answer sheet has four ovals for each item, representing those four choices. If the two addresses are the same, darken oval A. If there is a difference in the street address only, darken oval B. If there is a difference in the ZIP code only, darken oval C. And if there is a difference in both the street address and the ZIP code, darken oval D.

| A. No Errors | B. Address Only | C. ZIP Code Only | D. Both |

    Set your timer for exactly 11 minutes. Turn the page when you are ready and begin.

Part A: Address Checking

A. No Errors	B. Address Only	C. ZIP Code Only	D. Both

	Correct List		**List to Be Checked**	
	Address	**ZIP Code**	**Address**	**ZIP Code**
1.	21-C Southern Lane Baltimore, MD	62571	21-C Southern Lane Baltimore, MD	65271
2.	123 Lyric Way Conyers, MS	18282	123 Lyric Way Conners, MS	18282
3.	200 W. Jannine Dr. Missoula, MT	30707	200 W. Jannine Dr. Missoula, MT	30307
4.	18 Champlaine Way Rustic, NV	42101	18 Champaine Way Rustic, NV	24101
5.	62159 Rodaja Parsimony, KS	33489-6215	62159 Rodaja Parsimony, KS	33489-6215
6.	21314 10th Ave. S. Kalama, WA	10873	21314 10th Ave. E. Kalama, WA	10873
7.	10 Chartres Blvd. #9 Bakersfield, CA	61828	10 Chartres Blvd. #9 Bakaesfield, CA	61828
8.	1671 Anacapa Drive Greenevale, VT	95673	1761 Anacapa Drive Greenevale, VT	96573
9.	7776 Jasmine Circle Hayden Lake, ID	25354	7776 Jasmine Circle Hayden Lake, ID	25534
10.	43-J Kington Way Scottsdale, AZ	33284	43-J Kington Way Scottsdale, AZ	33244
11.	101 Monmouth Ave. East Lansing, MI	30035	101 Monmouth Ave. East Lansing, MI	30035
12.	2111Vantage Drive Milwaukee, WI	20512	2211 Vantage Drive Milwaukee, WI	21502
13.	61 Rural Route 2 Hana, HI	11783	62 Rural Route 2 Hana, HI	11783
14.	12487 Mariscal Lane Las Vegas, NV	32421	12487 Mariscal Lane Las Vegas, NV	32421
15.	32 Paseo Hidalgo Lubbock, TX	88131	32 Paseo Hidelgo Lubbock, TX	88131
16.	156 Burwood Terrace Rogerston, KY	76540	156 Birwood Terrace Rogerston, KY	76540

A. No Errors	B. Address Only	C. ZIP Code Only	D. Both

| **Correct List** | | **List to Be Checked** | |
Address	**ZIP Code**	**Address**	**ZIP Code**
17. 66 W Crusado St Laramie, WY	23302	66 W Crusado St Laramie, WY	22302
18. 46 S Greenberry Way Inbetween, WV	68905	48 S Greenberry Way Inbetween, WV	68095
19. 1440 Live Oak Lane Pomoway, WA	43679	1440 Live Oak Lane Pomoway, WA	43679
20. P O Box 2501-C Taos, NM	23795-2501	P O Box 2501-C Taos, NM	23765-2501
21. 12 Sycamore Canyon Washington, NH	85716	12 Sycamore Canyon Washington, NH	85176
22. 123 Polka Place Chicago, IL	76308	123 Polka Place Chicaga, IL	76803
23. 12457 Industrial Ave Lake Placid, NY	68107	12547 Industrial Ave Lake Placid, NY	61807
24. 113 Horse Trade Gulch Inchaway, UT	35250	113 Horse Trade Gulch Inchaway, UT	35250
25. 652 Popenoe Rd Oak Ridge, TN	78259	652 Papenoe Rd Oak Ridge, TN	78259
26. 1352 E Smith St Hershey, PA	78489	1352 S Smith St Hershey, PA	78489
27. 23256 Zephyr Blvd Princeton, NJ	65757	23526 Zephyr Blvd Princeton, NJ	65757
28. 252 Morningside Lane Atlanta, GA	65742	252 Morningside Lane Atlanta, GA	65752
29. 434 S 154th St St Louis, MO	89754	434 S 154th St St Louis, MO	98754
30. 33448 N Albers Ave Chapel Hill, NC	97876	33448 N Albers Ave Chapel Hill, NC	97876
31. 1997 Delinda Lane Northtown, ME	88335	1967 Delinda Lane Northtown, ME	88385
32. 197-B Oglesby Ave Cleveland, OH	68487	197-B Oglesbey Ave Cleveland, OH	68487
33. 8367 South Hills Lane Wetumpka, AL	48723-8367	8367 South Hills Lane Wetumpka, AL	48732-8367
34. 1009 W 49th Place Alacaseeli, RI	76892	1009 W 49th Place Alacaseali, RI	76892

A. No Errors	B. Address Only	C. ZIP Code Only	D. Both

Correct List		**List to Be Checked**	
Address	**ZIP Code**	**Address**	**ZIP Code**
35. 76 Buccaneer Circle Tampa, FL	55809	76 Buccaneer Circle Tampa, FL	25809
36. 889½ Glendower Dr Sand Hill, SC	49792	889½ Glenndower Dr Sand Hill, SC	79492
37. 67 Voorhees St Boston, MA	98789	67 Voorheese St Boston, MA	97889
38. 101 Via Margarita Telluride, CO	92131	101 Via Margarita Telluride, CO	92131
39. 42-B Jambalaya Lane Baton Rouge, LA	62268	42-B Jamalaya Lane Baton Rouge, LA	62268
40. 9434 Donington St Juneau, AK	21318	9484 Donington St Juneau, AK	21318
41. 87321 Bennington Ave South Bend, IN	42782	87321 Bennington Ave South Bend, IN	42872
42. 233½ Dorian Way Little Rock, AR	70206	233½ Dorian Way Little Rock, AR	70026
43. 25673 92nd St Dallas, TX	21342	25673 92nd St Dallas, TX	23142
44. 6667 Sprague St Minneapolis, MN	62597	6667 Sprague St Minneapolis, MN	62597
45. 291 Cedarbrooke Dr Gold Mountain, ND	89292	291 Cedarbrooke Dr Gold Mountain, ND	89292
46. 2912 Stafford Lane Highpoint, NB	31415	2912 Staford Lane Highpoint NB	41315
47. 3325 Granite Way Yipsivich, IA	97875	3325 Granite Way Yipsevich, IA	97875
48. 22 W Harvey, Apt. 3 Sauvage, SD	24136	22 W Harvey, Apt. 3 Sauvage, SD	23146
49. 99 Alpen Drive Yodelaihe, CO	86742	99 Alpen Drive. Yodliahe, CO	84762
50. 2357 Edam Terrace Holland, MI	22454	2357 Edam Terrace Holland, MI	24254
51. 1030 Eugenia Ave. Dover, DE	68768	1030 Eugenia Ave. Dover, DE	69768
52. 78469 Canal St Venice, CA	98564	78496 Canal St Venice, CA	98564

A. No Errors	B. Address Only	C. ZIP Code Only	D. Both

Correct List		List to Be Checked	
Address	**ZIP Code**	**Address**	**ZIP Code**
53. 776 16th Ave S Birmingham, AL	75683	776 16th Ave S Birminghem, AL	75683
54. 86743 Foxtail Drive West Farland, TX	55893	86743 Foxtail Drive West Farland, TX	55893
55. 337 Rural Route 6 Icebound, WI	32978	377 Rural Route 6 Icebound, WI	32798
56. 582 Friarstone Ct Kissimmee, FL	78238	582 Fiarstone Ct Kissimmee, FL	78328
57. 66 E Avenue P Johnson City, NV	27864	66 E Avenue P Johnson City, NV	26874
58. 74-B Concourse Ave Chicago, IL	77293	74-B Concoarse Ave Chicago, IL	77293
59. 23078 Greasewood Ln Kalamazoo, MI	45250	23078 Greasewood Ln Kalamazoo, MI	45250
60. 993 Koudekirk Drive Avalanche, MT	37826	993 Koudekirk Drive Avelanche, MT	37826

This is the end of Part A: Address Checking Section, Practice Test 2.

Part B: Forms Completion

Part B consists of 30 questions that test your ability to identify the information needed to correctly complete various U.S. Postal Service forms. You will be shown 5 different forms, each followed by 6 questions.

Set your timer for exactly 15 minutes. Turn the page and begin when you are ready.

Part B: Forms Completion

Insured Mail Receipt

Postage	**1.** $	☐ Fragile ☐ Perishable ☐ Liquid
Insurance Fee	**2a.** $	**2b.** Insurance Coverage:
Restricted Delivery Fee	**3.** $	
Special Handling Fee	**4.** $	
Return Receipt Fee	**5.** $	Postmark Here
Total Postage & Fees	**6.** $	
7. *Sent to:*		
8. *Street, Apt. No., or PO Box No.*		
9. *City, State, ZIP + 4, Country*		

Part B: Forms Completion

1. In which box would the total fees and postage be stated?
   A. Box 1
   B. Box 2b
   C. Box 4
   D. Box 6

2. What would indicate that the insured package contains perishable material?
   A. A check mark in the box next to Fragile
   B. A signature in Box 7
   C. A check mark in the box next to Perishable
   D. All of the above

3. In which box would China be an appropriate entry?
   A. Box 2a
   B. Box 2b
   C. Box 7
   D. Box 9

4. What would be a correct entry for Box 8?
   A. 3100 N. Olive Avenue
   B. $14.78
   C. DeKalb, IL 60115
   D. 818-555-1234

5. Luis Aspera is insuring his package, which is worth $200. Where would you indicate this?
   A. Box 1
   B. Box 2a
   C. Box 2b
   D. Box 5

6. In which of these should a person's or a company's name be entered?
   A. Box 3
   B. Box 7
   C. Box 8
   D. Box 9

Part B: Forms Completion

Certificate of Bulk Mailing

Fee for Certificate		1. [Current Rate Chart Here]	2. Meter stamp or postage stamps to be affixed here, and cancelled by postmarking with date.
	Up to 1,000 pieces		
For each additional 1,000 pieces or fraction thereof			

3a. Number of indentical pieces	3b. Class of mail	3c. Postage on each	3d. Number of pieces per lb.	3e. Total number of lbs.	3f. Total postage paid	3g. Fee paid

Postmaster's Certificate: I hereby certify that the above-described mailing has been received and number of pieces and postage verified.

4. Signature and Date _____

Part B: Forms Completion

7. How would you indicate that there are 6,500 identical pieces in this bulk mailing?
   A. Enter 6,500 in Box 2
   B. Enter 6,500 in Box 3a
   C. Enter 6,500 in Box 3d
   D. Enter 6,500 in Box 3f

8. Which of the following would be an appropriate entry for Box 3d?
   A. Drew Evans
   B. 1025 Stratford Lane
   C. 20
   D. A check mark

9. Which of these would be an acceptable entry for Box 3g?
   A. $25.00
   B. 80967-0012
   C. 5/11/06
   D. 60

10. Where does the Postmaster sign the form?
    A. Box 2
    B. Box 3g
    C. Line 4
    D. On the reverse side

11. Total Health Corp. is sending its bulk mailing as 1st class mail. Where would you indicate this?
    A. Box 1
    B. Box 2
    C. Box 3a
    D. Box 3b

12. Which of the following is an acceptable entry for Box 2?
    A. A signature
    B. A street address
    C. The number of pieces per pound
    D. A meter stamp

Part B: Forms Completion

Return Receipt for International Mail

<table>
<tr><td rowspan="6" style="writing-mode:vertical">Completed by office of origin</td><td colspan="3"></td></tr>
<tr><td colspan="3">1. Item Description:
☐ Registered Article   ☐ Letter   ☐ Printed Matter   ☐ Other</td></tr>
<tr><td>2a. ☐ Insured Parcel</td><td>2b. Insured Value</td><td>2c. Article Number</td></tr>
<tr><td colspan="2">3a. Office of Mailing</td><td>3b. Date of Posting</td></tr>
<tr><td colspan="3">4. Addressee Name or Firm</td></tr>
<tr><td colspan="3">5. Street and No.</td></tr>
<tr><td colspan="3">6. Place and Country</td></tr>
<tr><td rowspan="3" style="writing-mode:vertical">Completed at destination</td><td colspan="2">7. Postmark of the Office of Destination</td><td>8. ☐ The article mentioned above was duly delivered.</td></tr>
<tr><td colspan="2">9a. Signature of Addressee</td><td>9b. Date</td></tr>
<tr><td colspan="3">10. Office of Destination Employee Signature</td></tr>
</table>

Part B: Forms Completion

13. The parcel's value is $125. Where would you enter this if the parcel is insured?
   A. Box 1
   B. Box 2b
   C. Boxes 2b and 2c
   D. Box 9b

14. In which place(s) would 03/03/06 be a possible entry?
   A. Box 3b
   B. Boxes 3a and 3b
   C. Box 9b
   D. Boxes 3b and 9b

15. For which of these would "Austin, TX 78735-1751 U.S.A." be an appropriate entry?
   A. Box 6
   B. Box 6b
   C. Box 7
   D. None of the above

16. How should it be noted that the item mailed is a registered article?
   A. Make a note in Box 1
   B. Check "Registered Article" in Box 1
   C. Check "Registered Article" in Box 8
   D. Have the addressee sign in Box 9a

17. The Post Office where the article is to be delivered to is Trenton, New Jersey. Where would you indicate this?
   A. There is no place for this entry.
   B. Box 3a
   C. Box 4
   D. Box 7

18. Where does a postal representative's signature go on this form?
   A. Box 7
   B. Box 9a
   C. Box 10
   D. A postal representative's signature is not requested on this form.

Part B: Forms Completion

Customs Declaration and Dispatch Note

From			
Sender's Name			
Business			
Street			
City	State	ZIP Code®	
Country			

To		
Addressee's Name		
Business		
Street		
Postcode	City	
Country		

Detailed Description of Contents (1)	Qty. (2)	Net Weight (3) lb. oz.	Value (US $) (5)	For Commercial Senders Only	
				HS tariff number (7)	Country of origin of goods (8)

Check One ☐ Airmail/Priority ☐ Surface/Nonpriority	Total Gross Wt. (4)	Total Value (6)	Postage and Fees (9)

Check One (10) ☐ Gift ☐ Commercial sample ☐ Other	Sender's Instructions in Case of Nondelivery (16)	Mailing Office Date Stamp
☐ Documents ☐ Returned goods Explanation:	☐ Treat as Abandoned	
Comments (11) (e.g., goods subject to quarantine, sanitary/phytosanitary inspection, or other restrictions)	☐ Return to Sender - NOTE: Item subject to return charges at sender's expense.	

License Number(s) (12)	Certificate Number(s) (13)	Invoice Number (14)	☐ Redirect to Address Below:

I certify that the particulars given in this customs declaration are correct and that this item does not contain any dangerous article prohibited by legislation or by postal or customs regulations.	Date and sender's signature (15)

Part B: Forms Completion

19. Which of these would be an appropriate entry for Box 4?
    A. Susan Castle
    B. 65 lb. 8 oz.
    C. 36 bracelets
    D. $142.33

20. Where would you enter the following: 10 glass perfume bottles, 5 inlaid hand mirrors, 6 lacquered scissors?
    A. Box 1
    B. Box 3
    C. Box 5
    D. None of these

21. Where would you indicate that the total value of 10 glass perfume bottles, 5 inlaid hand mirrors, 6 lacquered scissors is $540?
    A. Box 1
    B. Box 5
    C. Box 6
    D. Box 9

22. Which of the following would be an acceptable entry for Box 2?
    A. 2 dz.
    B. $339.86
    C. 18 lb., 3 oz.
    D. Gift

23. Where would you list the monetary value in U.S. dollars of each item?
    A. Box 1
    B. Box 2
    C. Box 5
    D. Box 7

24. How would you indicate that the package is a commercial sample?
    A. Make a note in Box 1
    B. Write the license number in Box 12
    C. Check the "Surface/Nonpriority" box
    D. None of the above

Part B: Forms Completion

Return Receipt for Merchandise

Postage	**1.** $		
Return Receipt for Merchandise Fee	**3.** $		**2.** [PLACE POSTMARK HERE]
Special Handling Fee	**4.** $		
Total Postage & Fees	**5.** $		

6. *Waiver of Signature:* ☐ Yes   ☐ No

7. Recipient's Name (*PLEASE PRINT CLEARLY*)

8. Street, Apt. No., or PO Box No.

9. City, State, ZIP + 4

Part B: Forms Completion

25. In which box would the postmark be placed?
   A. Box 1
   B. Box 6
   C. Box 10
   D. None of the above

26. Where would a check mark be acceptable?
   A. Box 2
   B. Box 6
   C. Boxes 6 and 8
   D. Box 9

27. In Box 8, which of the following would be an acceptable entry?
   A. Mr. Tomoyuki Asai
   B. 351 East 85th Street, Apt 3F
   C. 2:35 pm
   D. 91001-4216

28. The Return Receipt Merchandise Fee is $1.50. Where would you indicate this?
   A. Box 3
   B. Box 4
   C. Box 5
   D. Box 6

29. Helen Stapenhorst is the recipient. Where should her name and address be printed?
   A. Box 7
   B. Boxes 7 and 8
   C. Boxes 7, 8, and 9
   D. None of the above

30. You might enter a dollar amount in any of the following boxes EXCEPT
   A. Box 1.
   B. Box 2.
   C. Box 3.
   D. Box 4.

This is the end of Part B: Forms Completion, Practice Test 2.

Part C: Coding and Memory

Overview

In Part C you will need to work quickly and accurately, using one Coding Guide to answer questions in two separate sections, the Coding Section and the Memory Section.

Prior to the scored segments of both the Coding Section and the Memory Section, there are practice segments. This test will follow the same format.

The Coding Guide that is used throughout Part C consists of four delivery routes. Three of the routes have two or three address ranges associated with them, and the last route covers any address not within the other three routes.

Each question (item) in both the Coding Section and the Memory Section consists of an address. Your job is to determine which of the four routes a given address belongs to and to mark your answer sheet accordingly.

In the Coding Section you may use the Coding Guide to determine the correct route for each address. In the Memory Section you will see exactly the same type of questions that are in the Coding Section, but you will no longer be able to look at the Coding Guide. Rather, you must determine which of the four routes an address belongs to, using only your memory of the Coding Guide.

The scored portion of the Coding Section has 36 questions, and you have 6 minutes to answer them. Prior to the scored portion, you will have two opportunities to practice using the Coding Guide.

The scored portion of the Memory Section also has 36 questions and 7 minutes to answer them. It also provides you with two opportunities to study and memorize the Coding Guide, as well as a chance to practice answering questions without using the Coding Guide.

Part C: Coding Section

Part 1: Sample Questions

Instructions Answering the questions on the following pages will familiarize you with the format and timing of the questions in Part C: Coding Section. You will have 3½ minutes to answer 12 questions, using the Coding Guide displayed opposite the questions.

Mark your answers in the sample ovals and check your answers using the correct answers shown at the bottom of the same page.

Set your timer for 3½ minutes and turn the page when you are ready to begin.

Part C: Coding Section

Coding Guide	
Address Range	**Delivery Route**
200–499 S Bel Air Drive 12–178 N 122nd Street 49–671 Delaware	A
300–601 Walnut Lane 78–120 Chandler Blvd NE	B
78000–80000 Ridge Road. 600–629 Fairbanks Ave 221–243 Rural Route 1	C
Any mail that is not found in one of the above address ranges	D

Part C: Coding Section

Exercise 1: Sample Questions

	Address	Delivery Route			
1.	558 Delaware	A	B	C	D
2.	221 Rural Route 1	A	B	C	D
3.	386 S Bel Air Drive	A	B	C	D
4.	76 Chandler Blvd NE	A	B	C	D
5.	401 Walnut Lane	A	B	C	D
6.	628 Fairbanks	A	B	C	D
7.	79000 Ridge Road	A	B	C	D
8.	600 Walnut Lane	A	B	C	D
9.	144 N 122nd Street	A	B	C	D
10.	601 Fairebanks	A	B	C	D
11.	177 N 122nd Street	A	B	C	D
12.	78002 Ridge Road	A	B	C	D

Answers

1. A
2. C
3. A
4. D
5. B
6. C
7. C
8. B
9. A
10. D
11. A
12. C

Part C: Coding Section

Coding Practice Test 2

Instructions   This section follows the format of Postal Exam 473. There are 36 questions, and you will have 6 minutes to answer them. Each page of questions is displayed opposite the Coding Guide, which you may use to answer the questions.

You will score this section and use it to help determine your score on this practice test. Mark your answers on your Practice Test 2 Answer Sheet in the Coding Section of Part C.

Set your timer for 6 minutes and turn the page when you are ready to begin.

Coding Section: Practice Test 2

Coding Guide	
Address Range	**Delivery Route**
200–499 S Bel Air Drive 12–178 N 122nd Street 489–671 Delaware	A
300–601 Walnut Lane 78–120 Chandler Blvd NE	B
78000–80000 Ridge Road 600–629 Fairbanks Ave 22–243 Rural Route 1	C
Any mail that is not found in one of the above address ranges	D

Coding Section: Practice Test 2

Questions

	Address	Delivery Route			
1.	626 Fairbanks Ave	(A)	(B)	(C)	(D)
2.	77 Chandler Blvd NE	(A)	(B)	(C)	(D)
3.	601 Walnut Lane	(A)	(B)	(C)	(D)
4.	119 Chandler Blvd NE	(A)	(B)	(C)	(D)
5.	14 N 122nd Street	(A)	(B)	(C)	(D)
6.	79010 Ridge Road	(A)	(B)	(C)	(D)
7.	222 Rural Route 1	(A)	(B)	(C)	(D)
8.	490 Delaware	(A)	(B)	(C)	(D)
9.	681 Delaware	(A)	(B)	(C)	(D)
10.	619 Fairbanks Ave	(A)	(B)	(C)	(D)
11.	119 Chandler Blvd NE	(A)	(B)	(C)	(D)
12.	202 S Bel Air Drive	(A)	(B)	(C)	(D)
13.	177 N 122nd Street	(A)	(B)	(C)	(D)
14.	495 Delaware	(A)	(B)	(C)	(D)
15.	7800 Ridge Road	(A)	(B)	(C)	(D)
16.	528 Walnut Lane	(A)	(B)	(C)	(D)
17.	234 Rural Route 1	(A)	(B)	(C)	(D)
18.	78 Chandler Blvd SE	(A)	(B)	(C)	(D)
19.	599 Walnut Lane	(A)	(B)	(C)	(D)
20.	610 Fairbanks Ave	(A)	(B)	(C)	(D)

Coding Guide	
Address Range	**Delivery Route**
200–499 S Bel Air Drive 12–178 N 122nd Street 489–671 Delaware	A
300–601 Walnut Lane 78–120 Chandler Blvd NE	B
78000–80000 Ridge Road 600–629 Fairbanks Ave 221–243 Rural Route 1	C
Any mail that is not found in one of the above address ranges	D

21.	79779 Ridge Road	Ⓐ	Ⓑ	Ⓒ	Ⓓ
22.	16 N 122nd Street	Ⓐ	Ⓑ	Ⓒ	Ⓓ
23.	253 Rural Route 1	Ⓐ	Ⓑ	Ⓒ	Ⓓ
24.	701 Walnut Lane	Ⓐ	Ⓑ	Ⓒ	Ⓓ
25.	101 Chandler Blvd NE	Ⓐ	Ⓑ	Ⓒ	Ⓓ
26.	411 S Bel Air Drive	Ⓐ	Ⓑ	Ⓒ	Ⓓ
27.	142 N 122nd Street	Ⓐ	Ⓑ	Ⓒ	Ⓓ
28.	622 Fairbanks Ave	Ⓐ	Ⓑ	Ⓒ	Ⓓ
29.	222 W Bel Air Drive	Ⓐ	Ⓑ	Ⓒ	Ⓓ
30.	626 Fairbanks Ave	Ⓐ	Ⓑ	Ⓒ	Ⓓ
31.	311 Walnut Lane	Ⓐ	Ⓑ	Ⓒ	Ⓓ
32.	96 Chandler Blvd NE	Ⓐ	Ⓑ	Ⓒ	Ⓓ
33.	505 Delaware	Ⓐ	Ⓑ	Ⓒ	Ⓓ
34.	233 Rural Route 7	Ⓐ	Ⓑ	Ⓒ	Ⓓ
35.	78050 Ridge Road	Ⓐ	Ⓑ	Ⓒ	Ⓓ
36.	613 Fairbanks Ave	Ⓐ	Ⓑ	Ⓒ	Ⓓ

This is the end of Part C: Coding Section, Practice Test 2.

Part C: Memory Section

Overview

There are four divisions in Part C: Memory Section. They are

1. a 3-minute period for studying the Coding Guide;
2. a 90-second nonscored practice, in which you answer 8 questions without using the Coding Guide;
3. a 5-minute period for studying the Coding Guide; and
4. a scored test, consisting of 36 questions, timed for 7 minutes.

During the two study periods there are no questions to answer; you are memorizing the Coding Guide. Section 2 is a timed practice test, with eight questions to answer in 90 seconds, and a sample answer sheet. Section 4 is the actual test. Use the Practice Test 2 answer sheet to mark your answers. They will be scored.

Memory Section: Part 1

Instructions

Part 1 of the Memory Section is a study period. Use it to memorize the Coding Guide. There are no questions to answer during the 3-minute study period.

   Set your timer for 3 minutes, and when you are ready to begin, turn the page.

Memory Section: Part 1

Coding Guide	
Address Range	**Delivery Route**
200–499 S Bel Air Drive 12–178 N 122nd Street 489–671 Delaware	A
300–601 Walnut Lane 78–120 Chandler Blvd NE	B
78000–80000 Ridge Road 600–629 Fairbanks Ave 221–243 Rural Route 1	C
Any mail that is not found in one of the above address ranges	D

Memory Section: Part 2

Instructions

In Part 2 of the Memory Section, you will practice answering questions using your memory of the Coding Guide (see p. 115), which will not be shown. This is only a practice exercise; it will not be scored.

Following the eight questions is a sample answer sheet that you will use to mark your answers. At the bottom of the page is the answer key for the sample questions.

Set your timer for 90 seconds; when you are ready, you may begin.

Memory Section: Part 2

	Address	Delivery Route			
1.	84 Chandler Blvd NE	(A)	(B)	(C)	(D)
2.	223 Rural Route 1	(A)	(B)	(C)	(D)
3.	303 Walnut Way	(A)	(B)	(C)	(D)
4.	670 Delaware	(A)	(B)	(C)	(D)
5.	230 Rural Route 1	(A)	(B)	(C)	(D)
6.	148 N 122nd Street	(A)	(B)	(C)	(D)
7.	404 Walnut Lane	(A)	(B)	(C)	(D)
8.	78060 Ridge Road	(A)	(B)	(C)	(D)

Answers

1. B
2. C
3. D
4. A
5. C
6. A
7. B
8. C

Memory Section: Part 3

Instructions

Part 3 of the Memory Section is a 5-minute study period. This is your final preparation period for the scored Memory test. Use it to finish memorizing the Coding Guide. As in Part 1 of this section, there are no questions to answer. Do not make marks of any kind during this study period.

Set your timer for 5 minutes, and when you are ready, turn the page and begin.

Memory Section: Part 3

Coding Guide	
Address Range	**Delivery Route**
200–499 S Bel Air Drive 12–178 N 122nd Street 489–671 Delaware	A
300–601 Walnut Lane 78–120 Chandler Blvd NE	B
78000–80000 Ridge Road 600–629 Fairbanks Ave 221–243 Rural Route 1	C
Any mail that is not found in one of the above address ranges	D

Memory Section: Part 4

Instructions

Part 4 of the Memory Section is the scored Memory test. You will have 7 minutes to answer the 36 questions, without using the Coding Guide. You must answer the questions from memory.

Mark your answers to these 36 questions on the Practice Test 2 Answer Sheet, using lines 37–72 of Part C: Coding and Memory. When you have finished, it is time to score the exam.

Set your timer for 7 minutes, and when you are ready, begin.

Memory Section: Practice Test 2

Questions

	Address	Delivery Route			
37.	599 Walnut Lane	(A)	(B)	(C)	(D)
38.	80 Chandler Blvd NE	(A)	(B)	(C)	(D)
39.	142 N 122nd Street	(A)	(B)	(C)	(D)
40.	691 Delaware	(A)	(B)	(C)	(D)
41.	607 Fairbanks Ave	(A)	(B)	(C)	(D)
42.	80000 Ridge Road	(A)	(B)	(C)	(D)
43.	237 Rural Route 1	(A)	(B)	(C)	(D)
44.	497 S Bel Air Drive	(A)	(B)	(C)	(D)
45.	108 Chandler Blvd NE	(A)	(B)	(C)	(D)
46.	211 Rural Route 1	(A)	(B)	(C)	(D)
47.	158 N 122nd Street	(A)	(B)	(C)	(D)
48.	625 Fairbanks Ave	(A)	(B)	(C)	(D)
49.	671 Delaware	(A)	(B)	(C)	(D)
50.	496 Walnut Lane	(A)	(B)	(C)	(D)
51.	120 Chandler Circle NE	(A)	(B)	(C)	(D)
52.	222 Bel Air Place	(A)	(B)	(C)	(D)
53.	118 Chandler Blvd NE	(A)	(B)	(C)	(D)
54.	111 N 122nd Street	(A)	(B)	(C)	(D)
55.	79101 Ridge Road	(A)	(B)	(C)	(D)
56.	513 Delaware	(A)	(B)	(C)	(D)

KAPLAN

57.	599 Walnut Lane	A	B	C	D
58.	306 Walnut Lane	A	B	C	D
59.	666 Delaware	A	B	C	D
60.	439 S Bel Air Drive	A	B	C	D
61.	13 N 122nd Street	A	B	C	D
62.	226 Rural Route 1	A	B	C	D
63.	707 Delaware	A	B	C	D
64.	598 Walnut Lane	A	B	C	D
65.	79904 Ridge Road	A	B	C	D
66.	610 Fairbanks Ave	A	B	C	D
67.	429 S Bel Air Drive	A	B	C	D
68.	117 Chandler Blvd NE	A	B	C	D
69.	159 N 122nd Street	A	B	C	D
70.	108 Chandler Blvd SE	A	B	C	D
71.	234 Rural Route 1	A	B	C	D
72.	572 Delaware	A	B	C	D

This is the end of Part C: Coding Section, Practice Test 2.

Part D: Personal Characteristics and Experience Inventory

As explained earlier, it is not possible to prepare for or practice the 236 job-related characteristics and experience questions in Part D. Therefore, no test items are included in this practice exam. For examples, please see Chapters 2 and 6.

Remember, there are no right or wrong answers in this section of Postal Test 473/473-C. Moreover, the USPS does not reveal how it evaluates the highly personal responses to Part D, nor how it weighs this part.

Feel confident that if you select the one response for each statement/question that best reflects your own personality, experience, and work ethics, you will be honestly representing yourself.

ANSWER KEY FOR PRACTICE TEST 2

Part A: Address Checking

1. C	25. B	49. D
2. B	26. B	50. C
3. C	27. B	51. C
4. D	28. C	52. B
5. A	29. C	53. B
6. B	30. A	54. A
7. B	31. D	55. D
8. D	32. B	56. D
9. C	33. C	57. C
10. C	34. B	58. B
11. A	35. C	59. A
12. D	36. D	60. B
13. B	37. D	61. A
14. A	38. A	62. C
15. B	39. B	63. D
16. B	40. B	64. B
17. C	41. C	65. C
18. D	42. C	66. C
19. A	43. C	67. A
20. C	44. A	68. B
21. C	45. A	69. A
22. D	46. D	70. D
23. D	47. B	71. C
24. A	48. C	72. A

Part B: Forms Completion

1.	D	11.	D	21.	C
2.	C	12.	D	22.	A
3.	D	13.	B	23.	C
4.	A	14.	D	24.	D
5.	C	15.	A	25.	D
6.	B	16.	B	26.	B
7.	B	17.	D	27.	B
8.	C	18.	C	28.	A
9.	A	19.	B	29.	C
10.	C	20.	A	30.	B

Part C: Coding and Memory

1.	C	25.	B	49.	A
2.	D	26.	A	50.	B
3.	B	27.	A	51.	D
4.	B	28.	C	52.	D
5.	A	29.	D	53.	B
6.	C	30.	C	54.	A
7.	C	31.	B	55.	C
8.	A	32.	B	56.	A
9.	D	33.	A	57.	B
10.	C	34.	D	58.	B
11.	B	35.	C	59.	A
12.	A	36.	C	60.	A
13.	A	37.	B	61.	A
14.	A	38.	B	62.	C
15.	D	39.	A	63.	D
16.	B	40.	D	64.	B
17.	C	41.	C	65.	C
18.	D	42.	C	66.	C
19.	B	43.	C	67.	A
20.	C	44.	A	68.	B
21.	C	45.	B	69.	A
22.	A	46.	D	70.	D
23.	D	47.	A	71.	C
24.	D	48.	C	72.	A

Postal Exam 473/473-C
Practice Test Answer Sheet

Tear out or photocopy one two-sided Answer Sheet for each Practice Test. This sheet is similar to the one you will mark at the real exam.

When taking the actual Test 473 or 473-C, you will first fill in the top half of the front side of the Answer Sheet, which asks for information similar to what you provided when applying for the exam. You will mark your answers for Address Checking and Forms Completion on the bottom half of the first side.

On the back side of the Answer Sheet, you will mark your answers for the final two sections of the test: Coding and Memory and Personal Characteristics and Experience Inventory.

For some excellent tips on marking your Answer Sheet, please see **Appendix A: Five Valuable Answer Sheet Marking Strategies** in the back of this book.

Part A: Address Checking

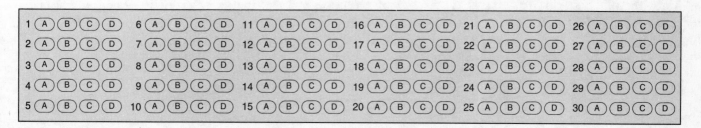

Part B: Forms Completion

continued on other side →

KAPLAN

Part C: Coding and Memory

Coding Section	Memory Section

Coding Section

1 Ⓐ Ⓑ Ⓒ Ⓓ   13 Ⓐ Ⓑ Ⓒ Ⓓ   25 Ⓐ Ⓑ Ⓒ Ⓓ
2 Ⓐ Ⓑ Ⓒ Ⓓ   14 Ⓐ Ⓑ Ⓒ Ⓓ   26 Ⓐ Ⓑ Ⓒ Ⓓ
3 Ⓐ Ⓑ Ⓒ Ⓓ   15 Ⓐ Ⓑ Ⓒ Ⓓ   27 Ⓐ Ⓑ Ⓒ Ⓓ
4 Ⓐ Ⓑ Ⓒ Ⓓ   16 Ⓐ Ⓑ Ⓒ Ⓓ   28 Ⓐ Ⓑ Ⓒ Ⓓ
5 Ⓐ Ⓑ Ⓒ Ⓓ   17 Ⓐ Ⓑ Ⓒ Ⓓ   29 Ⓐ Ⓑ Ⓒ Ⓓ
6 Ⓐ Ⓑ Ⓒ Ⓓ   18 Ⓐ Ⓑ Ⓒ Ⓓ   30 Ⓐ Ⓑ Ⓒ Ⓓ
7 Ⓐ Ⓑ Ⓒ Ⓓ   19 Ⓐ Ⓑ Ⓒ Ⓓ   31 Ⓐ Ⓑ Ⓒ Ⓓ
8 Ⓐ Ⓑ Ⓒ Ⓓ   20 Ⓐ Ⓑ Ⓒ Ⓓ   32 Ⓐ Ⓑ Ⓒ Ⓓ
9 Ⓐ Ⓑ Ⓒ Ⓓ   21 Ⓐ Ⓑ Ⓒ Ⓓ   33 Ⓐ Ⓑ Ⓒ Ⓓ
10 Ⓐ Ⓑ Ⓒ Ⓓ   22 Ⓐ Ⓑ Ⓒ Ⓓ   34 Ⓐ Ⓑ Ⓒ Ⓓ
11 Ⓐ Ⓑ Ⓒ Ⓓ   23 Ⓐ Ⓑ Ⓒ Ⓓ   35 Ⓐ Ⓑ Ⓒ Ⓓ
12 Ⓐ Ⓑ Ⓒ Ⓓ   24 Ⓐ Ⓑ Ⓒ Ⓓ   36 Ⓐ Ⓑ Ⓒ Ⓓ

Memory Section

37 Ⓐ Ⓑ Ⓒ Ⓓ   49 Ⓐ Ⓑ Ⓒ Ⓓ   61 Ⓐ Ⓑ Ⓒ Ⓓ
38 Ⓐ Ⓑ Ⓒ Ⓓ   50 Ⓐ Ⓑ Ⓒ Ⓓ   62 Ⓐ Ⓑ Ⓒ Ⓓ
39 Ⓐ Ⓑ Ⓒ Ⓓ   51 Ⓐ Ⓑ Ⓒ Ⓓ   63 Ⓐ Ⓑ Ⓒ Ⓓ
40 Ⓐ Ⓑ Ⓒ Ⓓ   52 Ⓐ Ⓑ Ⓒ Ⓓ   64 Ⓐ Ⓑ Ⓒ Ⓓ
41 Ⓐ Ⓑ Ⓒ Ⓓ   53 Ⓐ Ⓑ Ⓒ Ⓓ   65 Ⓐ Ⓑ Ⓒ Ⓓ
42 Ⓐ Ⓑ Ⓒ Ⓓ   54 Ⓐ Ⓑ Ⓒ Ⓓ   66 Ⓐ Ⓑ Ⓒ Ⓓ
43 Ⓐ Ⓑ Ⓒ Ⓓ   55 Ⓐ Ⓑ Ⓒ Ⓓ   67 Ⓐ Ⓑ Ⓒ Ⓓ
44 Ⓐ Ⓑ Ⓒ Ⓓ   56 Ⓐ Ⓑ Ⓒ Ⓓ   68 Ⓐ Ⓑ Ⓒ Ⓓ
45 Ⓐ Ⓑ Ⓒ Ⓓ   57 Ⓐ Ⓑ Ⓒ Ⓓ   69 Ⓐ Ⓑ Ⓒ Ⓓ
46 Ⓐ Ⓑ Ⓒ Ⓓ   58 Ⓐ Ⓑ Ⓒ Ⓓ   70 Ⓐ Ⓑ Ⓒ Ⓓ
47 Ⓐ Ⓑ Ⓒ Ⓓ   59 Ⓐ Ⓑ Ⓒ Ⓓ   71 Ⓐ Ⓑ Ⓒ Ⓓ
48 Ⓐ Ⓑ Ⓒ Ⓓ   60 Ⓐ Ⓑ Ⓒ Ⓓ   72 Ⓐ Ⓑ Ⓒ Ⓓ

Part D: Personal Characteristics and Experience Inventory

[When taking the real Test 473/473-C, you will mark the answers to the 236 questions in this area of the Answer Sheet.]

Part A: Address Checking

Instructions

Part A has 60 questions. You will have 11 minutes to complete this portion of the test. Each item (question) has two side-by-side addresses containing either identical or almost identical information.

You must compare each of the 60 items, decide if they are *exactly* the same or not, and mark the correct answers by blackening the corresponding ovals on your answer sheet. If the two addresses are different, you must decide if there is a difference in only the street address *or* in the ZIP code only *or* in both the street address *and* the ZIP code.

There are four answer choices, as you can see from the sample below; and the answer sheet has four ovals for each item, representing those four choices. If the two addresses are the same, darken oval A. If there is a difference in the street address only, darken oval B. If there is a difference in the ZIP code only, darken oval C. And if there is a difference in both the street address and the ZIP code, darken oval D.

A. No Errors   B. Address Only   C. ZIP Code Only   D. Both

Set your timer for exactly 11 minutes. Turn the page when you are ready and begin.

Part A: Address Checking

A. No Errors	B. Address Only	C. ZIP Code Only	D. Both

	Correct List		**List to Be Checked**	
	Address	**ZIP Code**	**Address**	**ZIP Code**
1.	19096 Barham Blvd Pierre, SD	26872	19096 Barham Blvd Pierre, SD	27862
2.	613-D Cedric Place Charleston, SC	87279	613-D Cedric Place Charleston, SC	87279
3.	399 Calzado Drive Albuquerque, NM	35202	399 Caldazo Drive Albuquerque, NM	32502
4.	9996 Alleluia Terrace Mt. Mystic, VA	78275	9996 Alleluia Terrace Mt. Mystic, VA	78275
5.	1616 Camarosa Santa Fe Springs, CA	21783	1616 Caramosa Santa Fe Springs, CA	21783
6.	1734½ W 53rd Ave Annendale-on-Hudson, NY	84732	1734¼ W 53rd Ave Annendale-on-Hudson, NY	84732
7.	2334 Glacier Circle Port Townsend, WA	42597	2334 Glacier Circle Port Townsend, WA	42957
8.	21178 Alsace Street Lincoln Park, CO	98465	21178 Alsace Street Lincoln Park, CO	98645
9.	1656 Chaparral Lane Carson City, NV	45354	1656 Chaparral Lane Carson City, NV	45354
10.	100374 Railroad Way Ann Arbor, MI	85756	10374 Railroad Way Ann Arbor, MI	85756
11.	1578 City View Drive Tucson, AZ	42578	1578 City View Drive Tucson, AZ	42578
12.	6878 Kukui Place Hakikianalei, HI	34842	6878 Kukui Place Hakikionolei, HI	34842
13.	86 Rural Route 3 Missoula, MT	53437	68 Rural Route 3 Missoula, MT	54347
14.	993½ MacArthur Drive Chevy Chase, MD	89683	993½ MacArthur Drive Chevy Chase, MD	89683
15.	P.O. Box 88187 Ft. Walton Beach, FL	68254	P.O. Box 88187 Ft. Walton Beach, FL	68524
16.	887 Wormstone Lane Bloomington, IN	93782	887 Wornstone Lane Bloomington, IN	93782

A. No Errors   B. Address Only   C. ZIP Code Only   D. Both

Correct List		List to Be Checked	
Address	ZIP Code	Address	ZIP Code
17. 45-A Eckelson St Rawlston, WY	47882	45-A Eckelston St Rawlston, WY	47782
18. 88 El Dorado Place Clark's Hollow WV	67938	88 El Dorado Place Clark's Hollow WV	67938
19. 4675 Andasol Ave Sycamore, AL	98458	4675 Andasol Ave Sycamore, AL	98548
20. 9150 Fuchsia Drive Asheville, NC	78425	9150 Freesia Drive Asheville, NC	78425
21. 41782 Hurley Hill Pass Fort Smith, AR	38967	41784 Hurley Hill Pass Fort Smith, AR	38967
22. 6565-B Rowhouse Ln Baltimore, MD	78256	6565-B Rowhouse Pl Baltimore, MD	78256
23. 34581 Old Fargo Hwy Kankolee, IL	82981	34581 Old Fargo Hwy Kankolee, IL	82891
24. 4528 Panther Paw Circle Franklin, TN	68928	4258 Panther Paw Circle Franklin, TN	69828
25. 62 N Gaffey Rd Eagle Creek, OR	33782	62 N Gaffey Rd Eagle Creek, OR	33782
26. 7825 S Suffolk Ln Oconichiwa, DE	95827	7825 N Suffolk Ln Oconichiwa, DE	95872
27. 82975 Gabbett Rd Dayton, OH	77372	82975 Gabbett Rd Dayton, OH	77372
28. 666-F Moreland Ave Atlanta, GA	83954	666-F Moreland Ave Atlanta, GA	83954
29. 8092 Montgomery St S Kansas City, MO	34542	8892 Montgomery St S Kansas City, MO	34452
30. 27 W Cragmont Pl Boise, ID	23923	27 W Craigmont Pl Boise, ID	23923
31. 150-C Mountain Drive Bar Harbor, ME	77843	150-C Mountain Lane Bar Harbor, ME	77843
32. 39082 W 53rd Ave Cedar Falls, IA	22821	39082 W 53rd Ave Cedar Falls, IA	22881
33. 2238 El Miradero Lane Austin, TX	19877-2238	2238 El Miradero Lane Austin, TX	19877-2238
34. 332 Star King Blvd Sacramento, CA	83702	332 Star King Blvd Sacramento, CA	83702

A. No Errors B. Address Only C. ZIP Code Only D. Both

Correct List		List to Be Checked	
Address	**ZIP Code**	**Address**	**ZIP Code**
35. P.O. Box 2249-A Biloxi, MS	78903-2249	P.O. Box 2249-A Biloxi, MS	78908-2249
36. 49½ Butterfield Terrace Jupiter, FL	29499	46½ Butterfield Terrace Jupiter, FL	29499
37. 1667 Camaloa Ave New Bedford MA	65855	1667 Cameloa Ave New Bedford, MA	65855
38. 7227 Lakeview Drive Saint Cloud, MN	21658	7727 Lakeview Drive Saint Cloud, MN	21568
39. 45-C Darkwood Drive Manhattan, KS	38729	45-C Darkwood Drive Manhattan, KS	38792
40. 33492 Lincolnshire Blvd South Burlington, VT	84692	33492 Lincolnshire Blvd South Burlington, VT	84692
41. 77 Tourmaline Road Metairie, LA	66763	77 Turmaline Road Metairie, LA	66763
42. 4589 Dollison Drive Nogales, AZ	27635	4589 Dollison Drive Nogales, AZ	27653
43. 973 Glennhill Lane Altoona, PA	47832	973 Glennhill Lane Altoona, PA	47832
44. 3784 Burrito Cir Tujunga, CA	84672	3874 Burrito Cir Tujunga, CA	84972
45. 4877 Calla Lily Ct Hannibal, MO	32428	4877 Calla Lily Cir Hannibal, MO	32428
46. 167 Inskeep Ave Waycross, GA	95758	167 Inskeep Ave Waycross, GA	95578
47. 966-D Jesslew St Dubuque, IA	22746	966-D Jesslew St Dubuque, IA	22476
48. 2772 Rural Route 4 Ketchikan, AK	13786	2722 Rural Route 4 Ketchikan, AK	18736
49. 8384 Indian Canyon Drive Stamford, CT	77485	8384 Indian Canyon Drive Stamford, CT	77485
50. 8832 Narcissus Crest Santa Barbara, CA	65893	8832 Narcissas Crest Santa Barbara, CA	65893
51. 223½ Rosabelle Rd Ogden, UT	34874	223½ Rosabella Rd Ogden, UT	34874
52. 31128 Walkatop Rd Harper's Ferry, WV	78927	31128 Walkatop Rd Harper's Ferry, WV	79827

A. No Errors	B. Address Only	C. ZIP Code Only	D. Both

Correct List		**List to Be Checked**	
Address	**ZIP Code**	**Address**	**ZIP Code**
53. 6726 Jonquil Field Ln Newport News, VA	81207	6726 Jonquil Field Ln Newport News, VA	81207
54. 81208 Avenue Q Narragansett, RI	48234	81308 Avenue Q Narragansett, RI	48324
55. 9956 Balzac St Pierre, SD	97476	9956 Balzec St Pierre, SD	97746
56. 44-C Phosphorous Ave Bowling Green, OH	75832	44-C Phosphorous Ave Bowling Green, OH	75382
57. 9937 Faulkner Lane Yazoo City, MS	64735	9937 Faalkner Lane Yazoo City, MS	64735
58. 65 Flaming Arrow Circle Nashua, NH	64724	65 Flaming Arrow Circle Nashua, NH	64724
59. 2393 Rensselaer Dr Perth Amboy, NJ	94734	2393 Renssalaer Dr Perth Amboy, NJ	94734
60. 6637 W 95th St Appleton, ME	57872	6637 W 95th Ave Appleton, ME	57827

This is the end of Part A: Address Checking Section, Practice Test 3.

Part B: Forms Completion

Part B consists of 30 questions that test your ability to identify the information needed to correctly complete various U.S. Postal Service forms. You will be shown 5 different forms, each followed by 6 questions.

    Set your timer for exactly 15 minutes. Turn the page and begin when you are ready.

Part B: Forms Completion

Authorization to Hold Mail

Postmaster, Please hold mail for:	
1a. Name(s)	**Note:** We can hold your mail for a minimum of **3 days**, but not for more than **30 days**.
2a. Address *(Number, street, apt./suite no., city, state, ZIP + 4)*	**2b.** I will pick up all accumulated mail when I return and understand that mail delivery will not resume until I do so. *Customer Signature* _____
3. Beginning Date	
For Post Office Use Only	
4a. Date Received	**4b.** PO ZIP Code
5a. Clerk	**5b.** Bin Number
6a. Carrier	**6b.** Route Number
Resumption of Mail Delivery	
☐ **7.** Accumulated mail has been picked up.	**8.** Resume Delivery of Mail *(Date)*
	9. By

Part B: Forms Completion

1. Where does the customer sign this form?
   A. Box 1a
   B. Box 2a
   C. Box 2b
   D. Box 9

2. Where is the bin number entered?
   A. Box 3
   B. Box 4a
   C. Box 5b
   D. Box 6b

3. In which box or boxes could 02/15/06 be an entry?
   A. Box 3
   B. Box 4a
   C. Box 8
   D. All of the above

4. What would indicate that the customer agrees to pick up the accumulated mail?
   A. A signature in Box 2b
   B. A date in Box 4a
   C. A check mark in Box 7
   D. All of the above

5. If Box 7 is checked, when can mail delivery resume?
   A. On the date in Box 3
   B. On the date in Box 4a
   C. On the date in Box 8
   D. On the date in Box 9

6. How many boxes require that a signature be entered?
   A. One
   B. Two
   C. Three
   D. Four

Part B: Forms Completion

Postage Statement - Special Services

Mailer Info.	Permit Holder's Name, Address, and Email Address, If Any	Telephone	Post Office of Mailing		Form Number of Attached Postage Statement	
			Mailing Date		**For Domestic**	**For International**
					☐ First-Class Mail	☐ Letter Post (LP)
			Permit Number		☐ Priority Mail	☐ Parcel Post (PP)
					☐ Standard Mail	☐ Express Mail (EMS)
			Statement Sequence No.		☐ Package Services	

■ Domestic Mail

		Service	DMM Section	Number Pcs. x	Fee	Totals
Special Services	A1	Certificate of Mailing *(Three or more)*	S914		$ 0.30	
	A2	Certified Mail	S912		$ 2.30	
	A3	Collect on Delivery (COD)	S921			
	A4	Delivery Confirmation	S918			
	A5	Insured Mail	S913			
	A6	Registered Mail	S911			
	A7	Restricted Delivery	S916		$ 3.50	
	A8	Return Receipt	S915		$ 1.75	
	A9	*Reserved*				
	A10	Return Receipt for Merchandise	S917		$ 3.00	
	A11	Signature Confirmation	S919			
Total Other Fees	A12	Parcel Airlift (PAL)	S930			
	A13	Special Handling	S930			
		Total Supplemental Postage *(Carry this amount to attached postage statement)* →				

■ International Mail

		Service	IMM Section	Number Pcs. x	Fee	Totals
Extra Services	B1	Insurance	320			
	B2	Recorded Delivery	360		$ 2.30	
	B3	Registered Mail	330			
	B4	Restricted Delivery	350		$ 3.50	
	B5	Return Receipt	340		$ 1.75	
Total		**Total Supplemental Postage** *(Carry this amount to attached PS Form 3651)* →				

Part B: Forms Completion

7. In which row would you insert information about Certified Mail?
- A. Row A1
- B. Row A2
- C. Row B2
- D. Row A4

8. What information would accurately go into the large "Mailer Info." Box in the upper left of this form?
- A. Permit holder's name
- B. Permit holder's address
- C. Permit holder's email address
- D. All of the above

9. There are 10 Domestic Mail/Restricted Delivery pieces. How much is the fee per piece?
- A. $1.75
- B. $2.30
- C. $3.50
- D. $35.00

10. If this form is used for international parcel post, where would you indicate that fact?
- A. With a signature in Row A12
- B. With a check mark in the "For Domestic" section
- C. With a check mark in the "For International" section
- D. That fact cannot be indicated on this form

11. Which service is represented in Row B3?
- A. Domestic Mail Registered Mail
- B. International Mail Insurance
- C. International Mail Recorded Delivery
- D. International Mail Registered Mail

12. What is COD an abbreviation for?
- A. Collect on Delivery
- B. Confirmation on Delivery
- C. Certified on Delivery
- D. Collect on the Docket

Part B: Forms Completion

Insured Mail Receipt

Postage	**1.** $	☐ Fragile ☐ Perishable ☐ Liquid
Insurance Fee	**2a.** $	**2b.** Insurance Coverage:
Restricted Delivery Fee	**3.** $	
Special Handling Fee	**4.** $	
Return Receipt Fee	**5.** $	Postmark Here
Total Postage & Fees	**6.** $	

7. *Sent to:*

8. *Street, Apt. No., or PO Box No.*

9. *City, State, ZIP + 4, Country*

Part B: Forms Completion

13. Margaret Clark is mailing a package that includes liquid soap and she has purchased $100 of insurance. Where would these facts be indicated?
    A. Boxes 1 and 2
    B. A check mark in the box next to "Liquid" and Box 2a
    C. A check mark in the box next to "Liquid" and Box 2b
    D. Boxes 2b and 7

14. For which of the following could $2.50 be an acceptable entry?
    A. Boxes 1 and 2a
    B. Box 3
    C. Boxes 3, 4, and 5
    D. All of the above

15. In which box would a special handling fee be indicated?
    A. Box 2b
    B. Box 4
    C. Boxes 4 and 5
    D. Box 10

16. Where would "Dr. Nancy Lu, America's Imports" be written?
    A. Box 7
    B. Box 8
    C. Box 9
    D. None of the above

17. Where would a ZIP Code + 4 be correctly entered?
    A. Box 2
    B. Box 7
    C. Box 9
    D. Box 8 or Box 9

18. Where does a postal clerk sign this form?
    A. Box 2b
    B. Box 7
    C. In the shaded box
    D. A postal clerk does not need to sign this form

Part B: Forms Completion

Customs Declaration

1. ☐ Gift ☐ Commercial Sample				
☐ Documents ☐ Other				
2a. Quantity and detailed description of contents:		**2b.** Weight lb. oz.		**2c.** Value (US $)
		3a. Total Weight		**3b.** Total Value (US $)
I, the undersigned, whose name and address are given on the item, certify that this declaration is true and correct and that this item does not contain any dangerous article prohibited by legislation or by postal or customs regulations.				
4a. Sender's signature				**4b.** Date

Part B: Forms Completion

19. Which of these would be an acceptable entry for Box 3b?
A. 12583 Morning Dew Way
B. $180.00
C. 91103-2610
D. A check mark

20. Molly Work is the sender. Where should her signature be entered?
A. Box 2a
B. Box 3a
C. Box 4a
D. Box 4b

21. The total weight of the contents is 3 lb. 12 oz. Where should this information be entered?
A. Box 1
B. Box 2b
C. Box 2c
D. Box 3a

22. Which of these would be an acceptable entry for Box 4b?
A. July 3, 2006
B. Certified Mail
C. A silver nut dish
D. None of the above

23. How would you indicate that documents are being mailed?
A. Check "Documents" in Box 1
B. Write "Documents" in Box 2a
C. Both A and B
D. None of the above

24. The parcel contains 2 books and 4 boxes of Swiss chocolate. Where should this be indicated?
A. Box 2a
B. Box 2b
C. Box 4a
D. Box 4b

Part B: Forms Completion

Domestic Return Receipt

SENDER: COMPLETE THIS SECTION	COMPLETE THIS SECTION UPON DELIVERY
■ Complete items 1, 2, and 3. Also complete item 4 if Restricted Delivery is desired. ■ Print your name and address on the reverse so that we can return the card to you. ■ Attach this card to the back of the mailpiece, or on the front if space permits.	A. Signature X ☐ Agent ☐ Addressee
	B. Received by (Printed Name) C. Date of Delivery
1. Article Addressed to:	D. Is delivery address different from item 1? ☐ Yes If YES, enter delivery address below: ☐ No
	3. Service Type ☐ Certified Mail ☐ Express Mail ☐ Registered ☐ Return Receipt for Merchandise ☐ Insured Mail
	4. Restricted Delivery? (Extra Fee) ☐ Yes
2. Article Number (Transfer from service label)	

Part B: Forms Completion

25. The addressee's signature goes where?
   A. Box 1
   B. Box A
   C. Box B
   D. Box 4

26. Which of these would be a correct entry for Box B?
   A. Marty Petrazini
   B. 10/21/05
   C. 3112 Burlington Avenue
   D. Yes

27. The delivery address is different from the one listed in Box 1. Where would you indicate this fact?
   A. A signature in Box A
   B. A check mark in Box 3
   C. A check mark in Box D
   D. A check mark in Box 4

28. How would COD service be noted?
   A. A check mark in Box A
   B. A check mark in Box D
   C. A check mark in Box 4
   D. None of the above

29. An agent is signing for this package. Where would that be indicated?
   A. A signature in Box 1
   B. A signature in Box A
   C. A check mark in Box 3
   D. A check mark in Box A

30. Which of these could be an appropriate entry for Box 2?
   A. 1DX5-13-84526
   B. Tim Healy
   C. August 3, 2006
   D. Certified Mail

This is the end of Part B: Forms Completion, Practice Test 3.

Part C: Coding and Memory

Overview

In Part C you will need to work quickly and accurately, using one Coding Guide to answer questions in two separate sections, the Coding Section and the Memory Section.

Prior to the scored segments of both the Coding Section and the Memory Section, there are practice segments. This test will follow the same format.

The Coding Guide that is used throughout Part C consists of four delivery routes. Three of the routes have two or three address ranges associated with them, and the last route covers any address not within the other three routes.

Each question (item) in both the Coding Section and the Memory Section consists of an address. Your job is to determine which of the four routes a given address belongs to and to mark your answer sheet accordingly.

In the Coding Section you may use the Coding Guide to determine the correct route for each address. In the Memory Section you will see exactly the same type of questions that are in the Coding Section, but you will no longer be able to look at the Coding Guide. Rather, you must determine which of the four routes an address belongs to, using only your memory of the Coding Guide.

The scored portion of the Coding Section has 36 questions, and you have six minutes to answer them. Prior to the scored portion, you will have two opportunities to practice using the Coding Guide.

The scored portion of the Memory Section also has 36 questions and seven minutes to answer them. It also provides you with two opportunities to study and memorize the Coding Guide, as well as a chance to practice answering questions without using the Coding Guide.

Part C: Coding Section

Part 1: Sample Questions

Instructions   Answering the questions on the following pages will familiarize you with the format and timing of the questions in Part C: Coding Section. You will have 3½ minutes to answer 12 questions, using the Coding Guide displayed opposite the questions.

Mark your answers in the sample ovals and check your answers using the correct answers shown at the bottom of the same page.

Set your timer for 3½ minutes and turn the page when you are ready to begin.

Part C: Coding Section

Coding Guide	
Address Range	**Delivery Route**
701–949 Randiwood Lane 18–399 E 47th Ave 501–800 Fairmount	A
222–710 Queen Anne 2800–3101 High Point St NW	B
33400–35600 Via Tivoli 58–99 Western Ave E 46–112 Rural Route 3	C
Any mail that is not found in one of the above address ranges	D

Part C: Coding Section

Exercise 1: Sample Questions

	Address	Delivery Route			
1.	566 Fairmount	(A)	(B)	(C)	(D)
2.	909 Randiwood Lane	(A)	(B)	(C)	(D)
3.	48 Rural Route 3	(A)	(B)	(C)	(D)
4.	220 Queen Anne	(A)	(B)	(C)	(D)
5.	703 Queen Anne	(A)	(B)	(C)	(D)
6.	34002 Via Tivoli	(A)	(B)	(C)	(D)
7.	2809 High Point St NW	(A)	(B)	(C)	(D)
8.	201 E 47th Ave	(A)	(B)	(C)	(D)
9.	98 Western Ave E	(A)	(B)	(C)	(D)
10.	110 Rural Route 2	(A)	(B)	(C)	(D)
11.	2900 High Point St NW	(A)	(B)	(C)	(D)
12.	610 Fairmount	(A)	(B)	(C)	(D)

Answers

1. A
2. A
3. C
4. D
5. B
6. C
7. B
8. A
9. C
10. D
11. B
12. A

KAPLAN

Part C: Coding Section

Coding Practice Test 3

Instructions   This section follows the format of Postal Exam 473. There are 36 questions, and you will have six minutes to answer them. Each page of questions is displayed opposite the Coding Guide, which you may use to answer the questions.

You will score this section and use it to help determine your score on this practice test. Mark your answers on your Practice Test 3 Answer Sheet in the Coding Section of Part C.

Set your timer for six minutes turn the page when you are ready to begin.

Coding Section: Practice Test 3

Coding Guide	
Address Range	**Delivery Route**
701–949 Randiwood Lane 18–399 E 47th Ave 501–800 Fairmount	A
222–710 Queen Anne 2800–3101 High Point St NW	B
33400–35600 Via Tivoli 58-99–Western Ave E 46–112 Rural Route 3	C
Any mail that is not found in one of the above address ranges	D

Coding Section: Practice Test 3

Questions

	Address	Delivery Route			
1.	35500 Via Tivoli	(A)	(B)	(C)	(D)
2.	394 E 47th Ave	(A)	(B)	(C)	(D)
3.	900 Fairmount	(A)	(B)	(C)	(D)
4.	909 Randiwood Lane	(A)	(B)	(C)	(D)
5.	610 Queen Anne	(A)	(B)	(C)	(D)
6.	18 E 47th Ave	(A)	(B)	(C)	(D)
7.	110 Rural Route 3	(A)	(B)	(C)	(D)
8.	35000 Via Tivoli	(A)	(B)	(C)	(D)
9.	3010 High Point St NW	(A)	(B)	(C)	(D)
10.	701 Fairmount	(A)	(B)	(C)	(D)
11.	940 Randiwood Lane	(A)	(B)	(C)	(D)
12.	20 E 47th Ave	(A)	(B)	(C)	(D)
13.	3000 High Point St SW	(A)	(B)	(C)	(D)
14.	66 Western Ave E	(A)	(B)	(C)	(D)
15.	701 Queen Anne	(A)	(B)	(C)	(D)
16.	888 Randiwood Lane	(A)	(B)	(C)	(D)
17.	2901 High Point St NW	(A)	(B)	(C)	(D)
18.	699 Queen Anne	(A)	(B)	(C)	(D)
19.	706 Fairmont	(A)	(B)	(C)	(D)
20.	99 Rural Route 3	(A)	(B)	(C)	(D)

KAPLAN

Coding Guide	
Address Range	**Delivery Route**
701–949 Randiwood Lane 18–399 E 47th Ave 501–800 Fairmount	A
222–710 Queen Anne 2800–3101 High Point St NW	B
33400–35600 Via Tivoli 58–99 Western Ave E 46–112 Rural Route 3	C
Any mail that is not found in one of the above address ranges	D

21.	2988 High Point St NW	(A)	(B)	(C)	(D)
22.	722 Randiwood Lane	(A)	(B)	(C)	(D)
23.	75 Western Ave E	(A)	(B)	(C)	(D)
24.	201 E 47th Ave	(A)	(B)	(C)	(D)
25.	3001 High Point St NW	(A)	(B)	(C)	(D)
26.	102 Rural Route 3	(A)	(B)	(C)	(D)
27.	34500 Via Tivoli	(A)	(B)	(C)	(D)
28.	910 Queen Anne	(A)	(B)	(C)	(D)
29.	940 Randiwood Lane	(A)	(B)	(C)	(D)
30.	92 Western Ave E	(A)	(B)	(C)	(D)
31.	2904 High Point St NW	(A)	(B)	(C)	(D)
32.	199 Western Ave E	(A)	(B)	(C)	(D)
33.	301 E 47th Ave	(A)	(B)	(C)	(D)
34.	102 Rural Route 3	(A)	(B)	(C)	(D)
35.	780 Fairmount	(A)	(B)	(C)	(D)
36.	32600 Via Tivoli	(A)	(B)	(C)	(D)

This is the end of Part C: Coding Section, Practice Test 3.

Part C: Memory Section

Overview

There are four divisions in Part C: Memory Section. They are:

1. a 3-minute period for studying the Coding Guide;
2. a 90-second nonscored practice, in which you answer 8 questions without using the Coding Guide;
3. a 5-minute period for studying the Coding Guide; and
4. a scored test, consisting of 36 questions, timed for 7 minutes.

During the two study periods there are no questions to answer; you are memorizing the Coding Guide. Section 2 is a timed practice test, with eight questions to answer in 90 seconds, and a sample answer sheet. Section 4 is the actual test. Use the Practice Test 3 answer sheet to mark your answers. They will be scored.

Memory Section: Part 1

Instructions

Part 1 of the Memory Section is a study period. Use it to memorize the Coding Guide. There are no questions to answer during the three-minute study period.

Set your timer for three minutes, and when you are ready to begin, turn the page.

Memory Section: Part 1

Coding Guide	
Address Range	**Delivery Route**
701–949 Randiwood Lane 18–399 E 47th Ave 501–800 Fairmount	A
222–710 Queen Anne 2800–3101 High Point St NW	B
33400–35600 Via Tivoli 58–99 Western Ave E 46–112 Rural Route 3	C
Any mail that is not found in one of the above address ranges	D

Memory Section: Part 2

Instructions

In Part 2 of the Memory Section you will practice answering questions using your memory of the Coding Guide (see p. 157), which will not be shown. This is only a practice exercise; it will not be scored.

Following the eight questions is a sample answer sheet that you will use to mark your answers. At the bottom of the page is the answer key for the sample questions.

Set your timer for 90 seconds; when you are ready, you may begin.

Memory Section: Part 2

	Address	Delivery Route
1.	695 Queen Anne	A B C D
2.	726 Randiwood Lane	A B C D
3.	51 Rural Route 3	A B C D
4.	708 Fairmount	A B C D
5.	68 Western Ave E	A B C D
6.	398 E 48th Ave	A B C D
7.	3100 High Point St NW	A B C D
8.	810 Randiwood Lane	A B C D

Answers

1. B
2. A
3. C
4. A
5. C
6. D
7. B
8. A

Memory Section: Part 3

Instructions

Part 3 of the Memory Section is a 5-minute study period. This is your final preparation period for the scored Memory test. Use it to finish memorizing the Coding Guide. As in Part 1 of this section, there are no questions to answer. Do not make marks of any kind during this study period.

Set your timer for 5 minutes, and when you are ready, turn the page and begin.

Memory Section: Part 3

Coding Guide	
Address Range	**Delivery Route**
701–949 Randiwood Lane 18–399 E 47th Ave 501–800 Fairmount	A
222–710 Queen Anne 2800–3101 High Point St NW	B
33400–35600 Via Tivoli 58–99 Western Ave E 46–112 Rural Route 3	C
Any mail that is not found in one of the above address ranges	D

Memory Section: Part 4

Instructions

Part 4 of the Memory Section is the scored Memory test. You will have 7 minutes to answer the 36 questions, without using the Coding Guide. You must answer the questions from memory.

Mark your answers to these 36 questions on the Practice Test 3 Answer Sheet, using lines 37–72 of Part C: Coding and Memory. When you have finished, it is time to score the exam.

Set your timer for 7 minutes, and when you are ready, begin.

Memory Section: Practice Test 3

Questions

	Address	Delivery Route			
37.	319 W 47th Ave	Ⓐ	Ⓑ	Ⓒ	Ⓓ
38.	929 Randiwood Lane	Ⓐ	Ⓑ	Ⓒ	Ⓓ
39.	99 Rural Route 3	Ⓐ	Ⓑ	Ⓒ	Ⓓ
40.	345 Queen Anne	Ⓐ	Ⓑ	Ⓒ	Ⓓ
41.	75 Western Ave E	Ⓐ	Ⓑ	Ⓒ	Ⓓ
42.	2850 High Point St NW	Ⓐ	Ⓑ	Ⓒ	Ⓓ
43.	700 Fairmount	Ⓐ	Ⓑ	Ⓒ	Ⓓ
44.	319 Queen Anne	Ⓐ	Ⓑ	Ⓒ	Ⓓ
45.	3560 Via Tivoli	Ⓐ	Ⓑ	Ⓒ	Ⓓ
46.	99 Western Ave E	Ⓐ	Ⓑ	Ⓒ	Ⓓ
47.	64 Rural Route 3	Ⓐ	Ⓑ	Ⓒ	Ⓓ
48.	616 Fairmount	Ⓐ	Ⓑ	Ⓒ	Ⓓ
49.	707 Randiwood Lane	Ⓐ	Ⓑ	Ⓒ	Ⓓ
50.	3030 High Point St NW	Ⓐ	Ⓑ	Ⓒ	Ⓓ
51.	725 Randywood Lane	Ⓐ	Ⓑ	Ⓒ	Ⓓ
52.	34440 Via Tivoli	Ⓐ	Ⓑ	Ⓒ	Ⓓ
53.	2978 High Point St NW	Ⓐ	Ⓑ	Ⓒ	Ⓓ
54.	299 E 47th Ave	Ⓐ	Ⓑ	Ⓒ	Ⓓ
55.	797 Fairmount	Ⓐ	Ⓑ	Ⓒ	Ⓓ
56.	3441 Via Tivoli	Ⓐ	Ⓑ	Ⓒ	Ⓓ

57.	111 Rural Route 3	Ⓐ	Ⓑ	Ⓒ	Ⓓ
58.	919 Randiwood Lane	Ⓐ	Ⓑ	Ⓒ	Ⓓ
59.	222 Queen Anne	Ⓐ	Ⓑ	Ⓒ	Ⓓ
60.	709 Queen Anne	Ⓐ	Ⓑ	Ⓒ	Ⓓ
61.	109 Rural Route 3	Ⓐ	Ⓑ	Ⓒ	Ⓓ
62.	303 E 47th St	Ⓐ	Ⓑ	Ⓒ	Ⓓ
63.	598 Fairmount	Ⓐ	Ⓑ	Ⓒ	Ⓓ
64.	3131 High Point St NW	Ⓐ	Ⓑ	Ⓒ	Ⓓ
65.	331 Queen Anne	Ⓐ	Ⓑ	Ⓒ	Ⓓ
66.	33500 Via Tivoli	Ⓐ	Ⓑ	Ⓒ	Ⓓ
67.	927 Randiwood Lane	Ⓐ	Ⓑ	Ⓒ	Ⓓ
68.	71 Western Ave E	Ⓐ	Ⓑ	Ⓒ	Ⓓ
69.	225 E 47th Ave	Ⓐ	Ⓑ	Ⓒ	Ⓓ
70.	2977 High Point St NW	Ⓐ	Ⓑ	Ⓒ	Ⓓ
71.	110 Rural Route 2	Ⓐ	Ⓑ	Ⓒ	Ⓓ
72.	572 Fairmount	Ⓐ	Ⓑ	Ⓒ	Ⓓ

This is the end of Part C: Coding Section, Practice Test 3.

Part D: Personal Characteristics and Experience Inventory

As explained earlier, it is not possible to prepare for or practice the 236 job-related characteristics and experience questions in Part D. Therefore, no test items are included in this practice exam. For examples, please see Chapters 2 and 6.

Remember, there are no right or wrong answers in this section of Postal Test 473/473-C. Moreover, the USPS does not reveal how it evaluates the highly personal responses to Part D, nor how it weighs this part.

Feel confident that if you select the one response for each statement/question that best reflects your own personality, experience, and work ethics, you will be honestly representing yourself.

ANSWER KEY FOR PRACTICE TEST 3

Part A: Address Checking

1.	C	21.	B	41.	B
2.	A	22.	B	42.	C
3.	D	23.	C	43.	A
4.	A	24.	D	44.	D
5.	B	25.	A	45.	B
6.	B	26.	D	46.	C
7.	C	27.	A	47.	C
8.	C	28.	A	48.	D
9.	A	29.	D	49.	A
10.	B	30.	B	50.	B
11.	A	31.	B	51.	B
12.	B	32.	C	52.	C
13.	D	33.	A	53.	A
14.	A	34.	A	54.	D
15.	C	35.	C	55.	D
16.	B	36.	B	56.	C
17.	D	37.	B	57.	B
18.	A	38.	D	58.	A
19.	C	39.	C	59.	B
20.	B	40.	A	60.	D

Part B: Forms Completion

1.	C	11.	D	21.	D
2.	C	12.	A	22.	A
3.	D	13.	C	23.	C
4.	A	14.	D	24.	A
5.	C	15.	B	25.	B
6.	B	16.	A	26.	A
7.	B	17.	C	27.	C
8.	D	18.	D	28.	D
9.	C	19.	B	29.	D
10.	C	20.	C	30.	A

Part C: Coding and Memory

1.	C	25.	B	49.	A
2.	A	26.	C	50.	B
3.	D	27.	C	51.	D
4.	A	28.	D	52.	C
5.	B	29.	A	53.	B
6.	A	30.	C	54.	A
7.	C	31.	B	55.	A
8.	C	32.	D	56.	D
9.	B	33.	A	57.	C
10.	A	34.	C	58.	A
11.	A	35.	A	59.	B
12.	A	36.	C	60.	B
13.	D	37.	D	61.	C
14.	C	38.	A	62.	D
15.	B	39.	C	63.	A
16.	A	40.	B	64.	D
17.	B	41.	C	65.	B
18.	B	42.	B	66.	C
19.	D	43.	A	67.	A
20.	C	44.	B	68.	C
21.	B	45.	D	69.	A
22.	A	46.	C	70.	B
23.	C	47.	C	71.	D
24.	A	48.	A	72.	A

Postal Exam 473/473-C
Practice Test Answer Sheet

Tear out or photocopy one two-sided Answer Sheet for each Practice Test. This sheet is similar to the one you will mark at the real exam.

When taking the actual Test 473 or 473-C, you will first fill in the top half of the front side of the Answer Sheet, which asks for information similar to what you provided when applying for the exam. You will mark your answers for Address Checking and Forms Completion on the bottom half of the first side.

On the back side of the Answer Sheet, you will mark your answers for the final two sections of the test: Coding and Memory and Personal Characteristics and Experience Inventory.

For some excellent tips on marking your Answer Sheet, please see **Appendix A: Five Valuable Answer Sheet Marking Strategies** in the back of this book.

Part A: Address Checking

1 Ⓐ Ⓑ Ⓒ Ⓓ	11 Ⓐ Ⓑ Ⓒ Ⓓ	21 Ⓐ Ⓑ Ⓒ Ⓓ	31 Ⓐ Ⓑ Ⓒ Ⓓ	41 Ⓐ Ⓑ Ⓒ Ⓓ	51 Ⓐ Ⓑ Ⓒ Ⓓ
2 Ⓐ Ⓑ Ⓒ Ⓓ	12 Ⓐ Ⓑ Ⓒ Ⓓ	22 Ⓐ Ⓑ Ⓒ Ⓓ	32 Ⓐ Ⓑ Ⓒ Ⓓ	42 Ⓐ Ⓑ Ⓒ Ⓓ	52 Ⓐ Ⓑ Ⓒ Ⓓ
3 Ⓐ Ⓑ Ⓒ Ⓓ	13 Ⓐ Ⓑ Ⓒ Ⓓ	23 Ⓐ Ⓑ Ⓒ Ⓓ	33 Ⓐ Ⓑ Ⓒ Ⓓ	43 Ⓐ Ⓑ Ⓒ Ⓓ	53 Ⓐ Ⓑ Ⓒ Ⓓ
4 Ⓐ Ⓑ Ⓒ Ⓓ	14 Ⓐ Ⓑ Ⓒ Ⓓ	24 Ⓐ Ⓑ Ⓒ Ⓓ	34 Ⓐ Ⓑ Ⓒ Ⓓ	44 Ⓐ Ⓑ Ⓒ Ⓓ	54 Ⓐ Ⓑ Ⓒ Ⓓ
5 Ⓐ Ⓑ Ⓒ Ⓓ	15 Ⓐ Ⓑ Ⓒ Ⓓ	25 Ⓐ Ⓑ Ⓒ Ⓓ	35 Ⓐ Ⓑ Ⓒ Ⓓ	45 Ⓐ Ⓑ Ⓒ Ⓓ	55 Ⓐ Ⓑ Ⓒ Ⓓ
6 Ⓐ Ⓑ Ⓒ Ⓓ	16 Ⓐ Ⓑ Ⓒ Ⓓ	26 Ⓐ Ⓑ Ⓒ Ⓓ	36 Ⓐ Ⓑ Ⓒ Ⓓ	46 Ⓐ Ⓑ Ⓒ Ⓓ	56 Ⓐ Ⓑ Ⓒ Ⓓ
7 Ⓐ Ⓑ Ⓒ Ⓓ	17 Ⓐ Ⓑ Ⓒ Ⓓ	27 Ⓐ Ⓑ Ⓒ Ⓓ	37 Ⓐ Ⓑ Ⓒ Ⓓ	47 Ⓐ Ⓑ Ⓒ Ⓓ	57 Ⓐ Ⓑ Ⓒ Ⓓ
8 Ⓐ Ⓑ Ⓒ Ⓓ	18 Ⓐ Ⓑ Ⓒ Ⓓ	28 Ⓐ Ⓑ Ⓒ Ⓓ	38 Ⓐ Ⓑ Ⓒ Ⓓ	48 Ⓐ Ⓑ Ⓒ Ⓓ	58 Ⓐ Ⓑ Ⓒ Ⓓ
9 Ⓐ Ⓑ Ⓒ Ⓓ	19 Ⓐ Ⓑ Ⓒ Ⓓ	29 Ⓐ Ⓑ Ⓒ Ⓓ	39 Ⓐ Ⓑ Ⓒ Ⓓ	49 Ⓐ Ⓑ Ⓒ Ⓓ	59 Ⓐ Ⓑ Ⓒ Ⓓ
10 Ⓐ Ⓑ Ⓒ Ⓓ	20 Ⓐ Ⓑ Ⓒ Ⓓ	30 Ⓐ Ⓑ Ⓒ Ⓓ	40 Ⓐ Ⓑ Ⓒ Ⓓ	50 Ⓐ Ⓑ Ⓒ Ⓓ	60 Ⓐ Ⓑ Ⓒ Ⓓ

Part B: Forms Completion

1 Ⓐ Ⓑ Ⓒ Ⓓ	6 Ⓐ Ⓑ Ⓒ Ⓓ	11 Ⓐ Ⓑ Ⓒ Ⓓ	16 Ⓐ Ⓑ Ⓒ Ⓓ	21 Ⓐ Ⓑ Ⓒ Ⓓ	26 Ⓐ Ⓑ Ⓒ Ⓓ
2 Ⓐ Ⓑ Ⓒ Ⓓ	7 Ⓐ Ⓑ Ⓒ Ⓓ	12 Ⓐ Ⓑ Ⓒ Ⓓ	17 Ⓐ Ⓑ Ⓒ Ⓓ	22 Ⓐ Ⓑ Ⓒ Ⓓ	27 Ⓐ Ⓑ Ⓒ Ⓓ
3 Ⓐ Ⓑ Ⓒ Ⓓ	8 Ⓐ Ⓑ Ⓒ Ⓓ	13 Ⓐ Ⓑ Ⓒ Ⓓ	18 Ⓐ Ⓑ Ⓒ Ⓓ	23 Ⓐ Ⓑ Ⓒ Ⓓ	28 Ⓐ Ⓑ Ⓒ Ⓓ
4 Ⓐ Ⓑ Ⓒ Ⓓ	9 Ⓐ Ⓑ Ⓒ Ⓓ	14 Ⓐ Ⓑ Ⓒ Ⓓ	19 Ⓐ Ⓑ Ⓒ Ⓓ	24 Ⓐ Ⓑ Ⓒ Ⓓ	29 Ⓐ Ⓑ Ⓒ Ⓓ
5 Ⓐ Ⓑ Ⓒ Ⓓ	10 Ⓐ Ⓑ Ⓒ Ⓓ	15 Ⓐ Ⓑ Ⓒ Ⓓ	20 Ⓐ Ⓑ Ⓒ Ⓓ	25 Ⓐ Ⓑ Ⓒ Ⓓ	30 Ⓐ Ⓑ Ⓒ Ⓓ

continued on the other side →

Part C: Coding and Memory

Coding Section

1 (A) (B) (C) (D)   13 (A) (B) (C) (D)   25 (A) (B) (C) (D)
2 (A) (B) (C) (D)   14 (A) (B) (C) (D)   26 (A) (B) (C) (D)
3 (A) (B) (C) (D)   15 (A) (B) (C) (D)   27 (A) (B) (C) (D)
4 (A) (B) (C) (D)   16 (A) (B) (C) (D)   28 (A) (B) (C) (D)
5 (A) (B) (C) (D)   17 (A) (B) (C) (D)   29 (A) (B) (C) (D)
6 (A) (B) (C) (D)   18 (A) (B) (C) (D)   30 (A) (B) (C) (D)
7 (A) (B) (C) (D)   19 (A) (B) (C) (D)   31 (A) (B) (C) (D)
8 (A) (B) (C) (D)   20 (A) (B) (C) (D)   32 (A) (B) (C) (D)
9 (A) (B) (C) (D)   21 (A) (B) (C) (D)   33 (A) (B) (C) (D)
10 (A) (B) (C) (D)   22 (A) (B) (C) (D)   34 (A) (B) (C) (D)
11 (A) (B) (C) (D)   23 (A) (B) (C) (D)   35 (A) (B) (C) (D)
12 (A) (B) (C) (D)   24 (A) (B) (C) (D)   36 (A) (B) (C) (D)

Memory Section

37 (A) (B) (C) (D)   49 (A) (B) (C) (D)   61 (A) (B) (C) (D)
38 (A) (B) (C) (D)   50 (A) (B) (C) (D)   62 (A) (B) (C) (D)
39 (A) (B) (C) (D)   51 (A) (B) (C) (D)   63 (A) (B) (C) (D)
40 (A) (B) (C) (D)   52 (A) (B) (C) (D)   64 (A) (B) (C) (D)
41 (A) (B) (C) (D)   53 (A) (B) (C) (D)   65 (A) (B) (C) (D)
42 (A) (B) (C) (D)   54 (A) (B) (C) (D)   66 (A) (B) (C) (D)
43 (A) (B) (C) (D)   55 (A) (B) (C) (D)   67 (A) (B) (C) (D)
44 (A) (B) (C) (D)   56 (A) (B) (C) (D)   68 (A) (B) (C) (D)
45 (A) (B) (C) (D)   57 (A) (B) (C) (D)   69 (A) (B) (C) (D)
46 (A) (B) (C) (D)   58 (A) (B) (C) (D)   70 (A) (B) (C) (D)
47 (A) (B) (C) (D)   59 (A) (B) (C) (D)   71 (A) (B) (C) (D)
48 (A) (B) (C) (D)   60 (A) (B) (C) (D)   72 (A) (B) (C) (D)

Part D: Personal Characteristics and Experience Inventory

[When taking the real Test 473/473-C, you will mark the answers to the 236 questions in this area of the Answer Sheet.]

PRACTICE TEST 4

Part A: Address Checking

Instructions

Part A has 60 questions. You will have 11 minutes to complete this portion of the test. Each item (question) has two side-by-side addresses containing either identical or almost identical information.

You must compare each of the 60 items, decide if they are *exactly* the same or not, and mark the correct answers by blackening the corresponding ovals on your answer sheet. If the two addresses are different, you must decide if there is a difference in only the street address *or* in the ZIP code only *or* in both the street address *and* the ZIP code.

There are four answer choices, as you can see from the sample below; and the answer sheet has four ovals for each item, representing those four choices. If the two addresses are the same, darken oval A. If there is a difference in the street address only, darken oval B. If there is a difference in the ZIP code only, darken oval C. And if there is a difference in both the street address and the ZIP code, darken oval D.

A. No Errors   B. Address Only   C. ZIP Code Only   D. Both

Set your timer for exactly 11 minutes. Turn the page when you are ready and begin.

Part A: Address Checking

A. No Errors	B. Address Only	C. ZIP Code Only	D. Both

	Correct List		List to Be Checked	
	Address	**ZIP Code**	**Address**	**ZIP Code**
1.	7821 W Alston Dr New Castle, DE	74895	7281 W Alston Dr New Castle, DE	77895
2.	44 Santa Fe Circle Pocatello, ID	25674	44 Santa Fe Circle Pocatello, ID	26574
3.	444514 Compound Blvd. Chicago, IL	65758	44514 Compound Blvd. Chicago, IL	65758
4.	265 Locust Ave Danville, KY	88967	265 Locast Ave Danville, KY	88967
5.	6672 Oakbar Rd Easthampton, MA	78394	6672 Oakbar Rd Easthampton, MA	78394
6.	33¹/₃ Windstar Pl. Roswell, NM	36173	33¹/₃ Windstar Pl. Roswell, NM	36713
7.	5527 Garrett St Sturgis, SD	42783	5527 Garrett St Sturgis, SD	42873
8.	21121 Farside Lane Knoxville, TN	78346	21211 Farside Lane Knoxville, TN	78346
9.	15-C Mirabeau Pl. Shreveport, LA	16176	15-C Mirrabeau Pl. Shreveport, LA	16716
10.	12489 153rd St. Hialeah, FL	66573	12489 153rd St. Hialeah, FL	66573
11.	77½ Exeter Drive Bridgeport, CT	75682	77½ Exeter Drive Bridgeport, CT	75982
12.	1990 Mahalo Lane Lahaina, HI	21573	1990 Mahalo Lane Lahaina, HI	27573
13.	993 Rural Route 1 Statesboro, GA	92724	933 Rural Route 1 Statesboro, GA	92724
14.	38674 Nashville Drive San Mateo, CA	31287	38674 Nashville Drive San Mateo, CA	31287
15.	P.O. Box 65257 Nogales, AZ	17717	P.O. Box 62527 Nogales, AZ	17177
16.	2257 Santoro Circle Texarkana, AR	32448	2257 Santoro Circle Texarkana, AR	32248

A. No Errors   B. Address Only   C. ZIP Code Only   D. Both

Correct List		**List to Be Checked**	
Address	**ZIP Code**	**Address**	**ZIP Code**
17. 2243 52nd Pl NE Tuscaloosa, AL	66475	2243 52nd Pl SE Tuscaloosa, AL	66475
18. 2157 Fairridge Dr. Grand Junction, CO	45752	2147 Fairidge Dr. Grand Junction, CO	45752
19. 8834 Poppyview Lane Frankfort, KY	77634	8384 Poppyview Lane Frankfort, KY	77634
20. 41675 225th St W Augusta, ME	89265	41675 225th St W Augusta, ME	89265
21. 224-B Rural Route 4 Seward, AK	23934	224-B Rural Route 4 Seward, AK	23943
22. 16675 Memorial Blvd Silver Spring, MD	66897	16675 Memoriam Blvd Silver Spring, MD	68897
23. 6775 Laredo Canyon Pass Winnemucca, NV	24559	6775 Laredo Canyon Pass Winnemucca, NV	24549
24. 18 S Ferdinand Glens Falls, NY	75875	18 S Ferdinand Glens Falls, NYy	78575
25. 177875 25th St W Kettering, OH	68283	177875 25th St W Kettering, OH	68283
26. 1667 Empalmo Ct West Warwick, RI	88956	1667 Empalmo Cr West Warwick, RI	88956
27. 88566 Blanche Rd Spartanburg, SC	52489	88556 Blanche Rd Spartanburg, SC	52489
28. 1664-C Eucalyptus Lane Burbank, CA	16782	1644-C Eucalyptus Lane Burbank, CA	16872
29. 6671 W Avenue Y St. George, UT	46758	6671 W Avenue Y St. George, UT	48758
30. 15 N Eastern Ave Kelso, WA	23923	15 N Eastern Ave Kelso, WA	23293
31. 18 Powder Horn Rd Oshkosh, WI	16867	18 Powder Horn Rd Oshkosh, WI	18687
32. 6622 Strawflower Ln Harper's Ferry, WV	83927	6622 Strawflower Ln Harper's Ferry, WV	83927
33. 1229 Winterwood Dr Erie, PA	66734-8264	1229 Winterwood Dr Erie, PA	66784-8264
34. 4171 Youngdale Lane Enid, OK	25346	4117 Youngdale Lane Enid, OK	25346

A. No Errors	B. Address Only	C. ZIP Code Only	D. Both

Correct List		**List to Be Checked**	
Address	**ZIP Code**	**Address**	**ZIP Code**
35. P.O. Box 18793 Chapel Hill, NC	72678	P.O. Box 18793 Chapel Hill, NC	72768
36. 677-B Timpangos Ter Duluth, MN	22847	667-B Timpangos Ter Duluth, MN	22847
37. 225 Nardian Way Pascagoula, MS	72974	225 Narnian Way Pascagoula, MS	72974
38. 28823 Doremus Road Hoover, AL	35728	28223 Doremus Road Hoover, AL	37528
39. 77 Hemmingway Lane Bowdoinham, ME	65234	77 Hemmingway Lane Bowdoinham, ME	65234
40. 1888 Laguna Circle Dr. Colorado Springs, CO	16128	1888 Laguna Circle Ct. Colorado Springs, CO	16128
41. P.O. Box 224 Greenwich, CT	65458-224	P.O. Box 224 Greenwich, CT	65485-224
42. 1657 Koopmans Court Dover, DE	45729	1657 Koopmann Court Dover, DE	47529
43. 1665 NE 268th Street Washington, DC	10459	1665 NE 268th Street Washington, DC	10549
44. 2398 Butterfield Rd Cape Coral, FL	57865	2398 Butterfield Rd Cape Coral, FL	57865
45. 109 Anabelle Ln Fort Wayne, IN	80902	109 Anabelle Ln Fort Wayne, IN	80902
46. 2420 E Cannon Ave Des Moines, IA	22891	2240 E Cannon Ave Des Moines, IA	22891
47. 8330 Van Gogh St St. Louis, MO	16748	8380 Van Gogh St St. Louis, MO	16748
48. 1441 Rural Route 4 Kalispell, MT	98274	1441 Rural Route 4 Kalispell, MT	98724
49. 1888 Quimby Road Cape May, NJ	83742	1888 Quimby Road Cape May, NJ	87342
50. 2231 Red Hat Canyon Alamogordo, NM	33798	2231 Red Hut Canyon Alamogordo, NM	33978
51. 2370½ Finley Ave Eugene, OR	28749	2370¼ Finley Ave Eugene, OR	28749
52. 2807 Quail Ridge Muskogee, OK	42975	2807 Quail Ridge Muskogee, OK	42795

A. No Errors	B. Address Only	C. ZIP Code Only	D. Both

Correct List		**List to Be Checked**	
Address	**ZIP Code**	**Address**	**ZIP Code**
53. 3327 Montara Drive Rutland, VT	78326	3327 Montera Drive Rutland, VT	78326
54. 299 W 16th Ave Olympia, WA	29748	299 W 16th Ave Olympia, WA	29748
55. 1673-C Olive St Richmond, VA	47829	1763-C Olive St Richmond, VA	47829
56. 442 Gallup Lane Lubbock, TX	29794	442 Gallup Lane Lubbock, TX	27974
57. 1776 Wright Ter Worland, WY	28483	1776 Wright Ter Worland, WY	28443
58. 1130 Juanita Way E Port Arthur, TX	84932	1130 Juanita Way W Port Arthur, TX	84932
59. 16674 Freshman Dr Columbus, OH	74846	1674 Freshman Dr Columbus, OH	74856
60. 6783 Valley Mall Passaic, NJ	78392	6783 Valley Mall Passaic, NJ	78392

This is the end of Part A: Address Checking Section, Practice Test 4.

Part B: Forms Completion

Part B consists of 30 questions that test your ability to identify the information needed to correctly complete various U.S. Postal Service forms. You will be shown 5 different forms, each followed by 6 questions.

Set your timer for exactly 15 minutes. Turn the page and begin when you are ready.

Part B: Forms Completion

Application for Post Office Box or Caller Service – Part 1

Customer: Complete items 1, 3-6

1. Name(s) to Which Box Number(s) Is (are) Assigned	2. Box or Caller Numbers _____ through _____
3. Name of Person Applying, Title *(if representing an organization)*, and Name of Organization *(if Different From Item 1)*	4a. Will This Box Be Used for: ☐ Personal Use ☐ Business Use *(Optional)*
5. Address *(Number, street, apt. no., city, state, and ZIP Code™)*. When address changes, cross out address here and put new address on back.	4b. Email Address *(Optional)* 6. Telephone Number *(Include area code)*

7. Date Application Received	8. Box Size Needed	9. ID and Physical Address Verified by *(Initials)*	10. Dates of Service _____ through _____

Part B: Forms Completion

1. Where should the entry "garretlang@axl.com" be placed?
   A. Box 1
   B. Box 3
   C. Box 4a
   D. Box 4b

2. Box 8 should contain what information?
   A. The box size needed
   B. The name of the person applying
   C. The dates of service
   D. The date the application was received

3. In which of these boxes would "Doug R. Kroker" be an appropriate entry?
   A. Box 1
   B. Box 2
   C. Box 5
   D. Either Box 1 or Box 3

4. Which of these would be an acceptable entry for Box 6?
   A. Yuri Zhivago
   B. 213-555-9876
   C. Thomas@earthconnex.net
   D. 61030-1124

5. Which of these would be an acceptable entry for Box 1?
   A. Yuri Zhivago
   B. 213-555-9876
   C. Thomas@earthconnex.net
   D. 61030-1124

6. In which box are entered the initials of the clerk who verifies the customer's ID?
   A. Box 2
   B. Box 4a
   C. Box 9
   D. There is no box for initials

Part B: Forms Completion

Delivery Type File Order Form

Customer Shipping Information		
1. Attention:		
2. Company:		
3a. Street Address, PO Box, Rural Hwy Contract Route and Box #:		**3b.** Apt/Suite #:
4a. City and State:		**4b.** ZIP + 4 :
5a. Foreign Country (*If applicable*):		**5b.** Foreign Postal Code (*If applicable*):
6a. Phone Number:	**6b.** FAX Number:	**6c.** Email Address:

Payment Method	
☐ Check ☐ Money Order ☐ Visa ☐ MasterCard ☐ American Express	Credit Card #: _____ Card Exp. Date: _____ Signature: _____

Part B: Forms Completion

7. Which of these could be an appropriate entry for Box 3b?
   A. 20A
   B. Scott McCullough
   C. $47.15
   D. Italy

8. Which of these could be an appropriate entry for Box 5a?
   A. 20A
   B. Scott McCullough
   C. $47.15
   D. Italy

9. What should you enter in Box 4b?
   A. Customer's telephone number
   B. Bin Number
   C. ZIP + 4
   D. Customer's Email address

10. The company name is America's Imports. Where should this be written?
   A. Box 1
   B. Box 3a
   C. Box 3b
   D. None of the above

11. How would you indicate that the customer is paying with Visa?
   A. By writing the credit card number on the correct line
   B. By making a check mark in the box next to "Visa"
   C. By writing "Visa" in the Payment Method box
   D. By signing the form

12. Where could a date like "02/09" be written?
   A. On the Card Exp. Date line
   B. In Box 4b
   C. In Box 5b
   D. On the Card Exp. Date line and in Box 6c

Part B: Forms Completion

Return Receipt for Merchandise

Postage	**1.** $	**2.** [PLACE POSTMARK HERE]
Return Receipt for Merchandise Fee	**3.** $	
Special Handling Fee	**4.** $	
Total Postage & Fees	**5.** $	

6. *Waiver of Signature:*   ☐ Yes   ☐ No

7. Recipient's Name (*PLEASE PRINT CLEARLY*)

8. Street, Apt. No., or PO Box No.

9. City, State, ZIP + 4

Part B: Forms Completion

13. A return receipt is being requested by sender Alyssa Bell from recipient Dr. Cranston Hayes of 6613 Oxley Rd., Santa Cruz, CA 95064-1118. Where should "Santa Cruz, CA 95064-1118" be entered?
   A. Box 7
   B. Box 8
   C. Box 9
   D. None of the above

14. A return receipt is being requested by sender Alyssa Bell from recipient Dr. Cranston Hayes of 6613 Oxley Rd., Santa Cruz, CA 95064-1118. Where should "Alyssa Bell" be entered?
   A. Box 7
   B. Box 8
   C. Box 9
   D. None of the above

15. A return receipt is being requested by sender Alyssa Bell from recipient Dr. Cranston Hayes of 6613 Oxley Rd., Santa Cruz, CA 95064-1118. Where should "Dr. Cranston Hayes" be entered?
   A. Box 7
   B. Box 8
   C. Box 9
   D. None of the above

16. In Box 5, which of the following would be a suitable entry?
   A. $17.89
   B. Kate Zhou
   C. 999 Westminster Circle
   D. Baltimore, MD 62571

17. The recipient's signature is being waived. Where would you indicate this?
   A. Box 2
   B. Box 5
   C. Box 6
   D. Box 9

18. What should be entered in Box 2?
   A. A check mark
   B. A postmark
   C. A Special Handling Fee
   D. A signature

Part B: Forms Completion

Express Mail Mailing Label

1a. Date Accepted Mo. Day Year	**1b.** Postage $
2a. Time Accepted ☐ AM ☐ PM	**2b.** Return Receipt Fee $
3a. Flat Rate ☐ or Weight lbs. ozs.	**3b.** COD Fee $	**3c.** Insurance Fee $
4a. PO ZIP Code	**4b.** Total Postage & Fees $
5. FROM: (PLEASE PRINT ADDRESS) PHONE ( ) _____	**6. TO:** (PLEASE PRINT ADDRESS) PHONE ( ) _____

Part B: Forms Completion

19. Where should the sender's name and address be entered?
    A. Box 1b
    B. Box 3c
    C. Box 4a
    D. Box 5

20. Where would a dollar amount be appropriately entered?
    A. Boxes 1b and 4b
    B. Boxes 1b, 2b, 3b, and 3c
    C. Boxes 1b, 2b, 3b, 3c, and 4b
    D. Boxes 1b, 2b, 3b, 3c, 4b, and 4c

21. Which of the following would be correctly entered in Box 2a?
    A. 10:32
    B. $10.32
    C. 10324-1780
    D. 10 lb, 3 oz

22. This Express Mail envelope is being sent COD. Where would the fee for this service be written?
    A. Box 2a
    B. Box 3b
    C. Box 3c
    D. Box 6

23. The recipient's phone number is 808-555-4411. Where would you indicate this?
    A. Box 4a
    B. Box 5
    C. Box 6
    D. None of the above

24. Into which boxes should a ZIP code be entered?
    A. Box 4a
    B. Box 5
    C. Box 6
    D. All of the above

Part B: Forms Completion

Customs Declaration

| 1. | ☐ Gift | ☐ Commercial Sample |
| | ☐ Documents | ☐ Other |

2a. Quantity and detailed description of contents:	**2b.** Weight		**2c.** Value
	lb.	oz.	(US $)
	3a. Total Weight		**3b.** Total Value (US $)

I, the undersigned, whose name and address are given on the item, certify that this declaration is true and correct and that this item does not contain any dangerous article prohibited by legislation or by postal or customs regulations.

4a. Sender's signature	**4b.** Date

Part B: Forms Completion

25. Which of these would be an acceptable entry for Box 3b?
  A. 2 lb, 14 oz
  B. Gift
  C. Louisa Trotter
  D. None of the above

26. What would be an accurate entry for Box 4a?
  A. A check mark
  B. A signature
  C. A weight
  D. An address

27. The total weight of four items in a package is 5 pounds 4 ounces. Where would this be noted?
  A. Box 1
  B. Box 2b
  C. Box 3a
  D. Both Boxes 2b and 3a

28. This package is a gift of hand crocheted lace from France. How should this be indicated on the form?
  A. Check "Gift" in Box 1
  B. Check "Gift" in Box 2a
  C. Write "Gift of lace" in Box 3a
  D. Sign Box 4a

29. Where would you list the monetary value of each item?
  A. Box 2a
  B. Box 2b
  C. Box 2c
  D. Box 3b

30. In which of these would "4 lb, 2 oz" be an acceptable entry?
  A. Box 2b
  B. Box 2c
  C. Box 2b and Box 3a
  D. All of the above

This is the end of Part B: Forms Completion, Practice Test 4.

Part C: Coding and Memory

Overview

In Part C you will need to work quickly and accurately, using one Coding Guide to answer questions in two separate sections, the Coding Section and the Memory Section.

Prior to the scored segments of both the Coding Section and the Memory Section, there are practice segments. This test will follow the same format.

The Coding Guide that is used throughout Part C consists of four delivery routes. Three of the routes have two or three address ranges associated with them, and the last route covers any address not within the other three routes.

Each question (item) in both the Coding Section and the Memory Section consists of an address. Your job is to determine which of the four routes a given address belongs to and to mark your answer sheet accordingly.

In the Coding Section you may use the Coding Guide to determine the correct route for each address. In the Memory Section you will see exactly the same type of questions that are in the Coding Section, but you will no longer be able to look at the Coding Guide. Rather, you must determine which of the four routes an address belongs to, using only your memory of the Coding Guide.

The scored portion of the Coding Section has 36 questions, and you have 6 minutes to answer them. Prior to the scored portion, you will have two opportunities to practice using the Coding Guide.

The scored portion of the Memory Section also has 36 questions and 7 minutes to answer them. It also provides you with two opportunities to study and memorize the Coding Guide, as well as a chance to practice answering questions without using the Coding Guide.

Part C: Coding Section

Part 1: Sample Questions

Instructions   Answering the questions on the following pages will familiarize you with the format and timing of the questions in Part C: Coding Section. You will have 3½ minutes to answer 12 questions, using the Coding Guide displayed opposite the questions.

Mark your answers in the sample ovals and check your answers using the correct answers shown at the bottom of the same page.

Set your timer for 3½ minutes and turn the page when you are ready to begin.

Part C: Coding Section

Coding Guide	
Address Range	**Delivery Route**
901–1349 Andalusia Way 101–499 W 63rd St 1200–1698 Grinnell Dr	A
310–990 Forest Lawn 16600–19998 Business Circle	B
2020–2187 Greystone Pl 322–601 S Pittsdale Hwy 21–145 Rural Route 2	C
Any mail that is not found in one of the above address ranges	D

Part C: Coding Section

Exercise 1: Sample Questions

	Address	Delivery Route			
1.	17892 Business Circle	A	B	C	D
2.	1401 Grinnell Drive	A	B	C	D
3.	99 Rural Route 2	A	B	C	D
4.	2106 Greystone Pl	A	B	C	D
5.	336 W 63rd St	A	B	C	D
6.	661 S Pittsdale Hwy	A	B	C	D
7.	778 Forest Lawn	A	B	C	D
8.	1010 Andalusia Way	A	B	C	D
9.	2140 Greystone Pl	A	B	C	D
10.	159 Rural Route 2	A	B	C	D
11.	16701 Business Circle	A	B	C	D
12.	1200 Grinnell Drive	A	B	C	D

Answers

1. B
2. A
3. C
4. C
5. A
6. D
7. B
8. A
9. C
10. D
11. B
12. A

KAPLAN

Part C: Coding Section

Coding Practice Test 4

Instructions   This section follows the format of Postal Exam 473. There are 36 questions, and you will have 6 minutes to answer them. Each page of questions is displayed opposite the Coding Guide, which you may use to answer the questions.

You will score this section and use it to help determine your score on this practice test. Mark your answers on your Practice Test 4 Answer Sheet in the Coding Section of Part C.

Set your timer for 6 minutes and turn the page when you are ready to begin.

Coding Guide	
Address Range	**Delivery Route**
901–1349 Andalusia Way 101–499 W 63rd St 1200–1698 Grinnell Dr	A
310–990 Forest Lawn 16600–19998 Business Circle	B
2020–2187 Greystone Pl 322–601 S Pittsdale Hwy 21–145 Rural Route 2	C
Any mail that is not found in one of the above address ranges	D

Coding Section: Practice Test 4

Questions

	Address	Delivery Route			
1.	381 W 63rd St	(A)	(B)	(C)	(D)
2.	2021 Greystone Ln	(A)	(B)	(C)	(D)
3.	1224 Andalusia Way	(A)	(B)	(C)	(D)
4.	552 S Pittsdale Hwy	(A)	(B)	(C)	(D)
5.	45 Rural Route 2	(A)	(B)	(C)	(D)
6.	989 Forest Lawn	(A)	(B)	(C)	(D)
7.	17856 Business Circle	(A)	(B)	(C)	(D)
8.	1356 Grinnell Dr	(A)	(B)	(C)	(D)
9.	323 S Pittsdale Hwy	(A)	(B)	(C)	(D)
10.	121 E 63rd St	(A)	(B)	(C)	(D)
11.	114 Rural Route 2	(A)	(B)	(C)	(D)
12.	2177 Greystone Pl	(A)	(B)	(C)	(D)
13.	1147 Andalusia Way	(A)	(B)	(C)	(D)
14.	1495 Grinnell Dr	(A)	(B)	(C)	(D)
15.	366 W 63rd St	(A)	(B)	(C)	(D)
16.	788 Forest Lawn	(A)	(B)	(C)	(D)
17.	1359 Andalusia Way	(A)	(B)	(C)	(D)
18.	16650 Business Circle	(A)	(B)	(C)	(D)
19.	558 S Pittsdale Hwy	(A)	(B)	(C)	(D)
20.	25 Rural Route 2	(A)	(B)	(C)	(D)

Coding Guide	
Address Range	**Delivery Route**
901–1349 Andalusia Way 101–499 W 63rd St 1200–1698 Grinnell Dr	A
310–990 Forest Lawn 16600–19998 Business Circle	B
2020–2187 Greystone Pl. 322–601 S Pittsdale Hwy 21–145 Rural Route 2	C
Any mail that is not found in one of the above address ranges	D

21.	783 Forest Lawn	(A)	(B)	(C)	(D)
22.	1170 Andalusia Way	(A)	(B)	(C)	(D)
23.	16579 Business Circle	(A)	(B)	(C)	(D)
24.	225 W 63rd St	(A)	(B)	(C)	(D)
25.	559 S Pittsberg Hwy	(A)	(B)	(C)	(D)
26.	18965 Business Circle	(A)	(B)	(C)	(D)
27.	777 Forest Lawn	(A)	(B)	(C)	(D)
28.	99 Rural Route 2	(A)	(B)	(C)	(D)
29.	1492 Grinnell Drive	(A)	(B)	(C)	(D)
30.	571 S Pittsdale Hwy	(A)	(B)	(C)	(D)
31.	845 Andalusia Way	(A)	(B)	(C)	(D)
32.	22 Rural Route 1	(A)	(B)	(C)	(D)
33.	18192 Business Circle	(A)	(B)	(C)	(D)
34.	323 N Pittsdale Hwy	(A)	(B)	(C)	(D)
35.	321 W 63rd Street	(A)	(B)	(C)	(D)
36.	2087 Greystone Place	(A)	(B)	(C)	(D)

This is the end of Part C: Coding Section, Practice Test 4.

Part C: Memory Section

Overview

There are four divisions in Part C: Memory Section. They are

1. a 3-minute period for studying the Coding Guide;
2. a 90-second nonscored practice, in which you answer 8 questions without using the Coding Guide;
3. a 5-minute period for studying the Coding Guide; and
4. a scored test, consisting of 36 questions, timed for 7 minutes.

During the two study periods there are no questions to answer; you are memorizing the Coding Guide. Section 2 is a timed practice test, with eight questions to answer in 90 seconds, and a sample answer sheet. Section 4 is the actual test. Use the Practice Test 4 answer sheet to mark your answers. They will be scored.

Memory Section: Part 1

Instructions

Part 1 of the Memory Section is a study period. Use it to memorize the Coding Guide. There are no questions to answer during the 3-minute study period.

Set your timer for 3 minutes, and when you are ready to begin, turn the page.

Memory Section: Part 1

Coding Guide	
Address Range	**Delivery Route**
901–1349 Andalusia Way 101–499 W 63rd St 1200–1698 Grinnell Dr	A
310–990 Forest Lawn 16600–19998 Business Circle	B
2020–2187 Greystone Pl 322–601 S Pittsdale Hwy 21–145 Rural Route 2	C
Any mail that is not found in one of the above address ranges	D

Memory Section: Part 2

Instructions

In Part 2 of the Memory Section you will practice answering questions using your memory of the Coding Guide (see p. 199), which will not be shown. This is only a practice exercise; it will not be scored.

Following the 8 questions is a sample answer sheet that you will use to mark your answers. At the bottom of the page is the answer key for the sample questions.

Set your timer for 90 seconds; you are ready, you may begin.

Memory Section: Part 2

	Address	Delivery Route			
1.	95 Rural Route 2	(A)	(B)	(C)	(D)
2.	309 Forest Lawn	(A)	(B)	(C)	(D)
3.	323 S Pittsdale Hwy	(A)	(B)	(C)	(D)
4.	1221 Grinnell Drive	(A)	(B)	(C)	(D)
5.	17294 Business Circle	(A)	(B)	(C)	(D)
6.	909 Forest Lawn	(A)	(B)	(C)	(D)
7.	1020 Andalusia Way	(A)	(B)	(C)	(D)
8.	2144 Greystone Pl	(A)	(B)	(C)	(D)

Answers

1. C
2. D
3. C
4. A
5. B
6. B
7. A
8. C

Memory Section: Part 3

Instructions

Part 3 of the Memory Section is a 5-minute study period. This is your final preparation period for the scored Memory test. Use it to finish memorizing the Coding Guide. As in Part 1 of this section, there are no questions to answer. Do not make marks of any kind during this study period.

Set your timer for 5 minutes, and when you are ready, turn the page and begin.

Memory Section: Part 3

Coding Guide	
Address Range	**Delivery Route**
901–1349 Andalusia Way 101–499 W 63rd St 1200–1698 Grinnell Dr	A
310–990 Forest Lawn 16600–19998 Business Circle	B
2020–2187 Greystone Pl 322–601 S Pittsdale Hwy 21–145 Rural Route 2	C
Any mail that is not found in one of the above address ranges	D

Memory Section: Part 4

Instructions

Part 4 of the Memory Section is the scored Memory test. You will have 7 minutes to answer the 36 questions, without using the Coding Guide. You must answer the questions from memory.

Mark your answers to these 36 questions on the Practice Test 4 Answer Sheet, using lines 37–72 of Part C: Coding and Memory. When you have finished, it is time to score the exam.

Set your timer for 7 minutes, and when you are ready, begin.

Memory Section: Practice Test 4

Questions

	Address	Delivery Route			
37.	44 Rural Route 2	(A)	(B)	(C)	(D)
38.	2022 Greystone Pl	(A)	(B)	(C)	(D)
39.	320 S Pittsdale Hwy	(A)	(B)	(C)	(D)
40.	1545 Grinnell Dr	(A)	(B)	(C)	(D)
41.	299 W 63rd St	(A)	(B)	(C)	(D)
42.	18843 Business Circle	(A)	(B)	(C)	(D)
43.	1369 Andalusia Way	(A)	(B)	(C)	(D)
44.	731 Forest Lawn	(A)	(B)	(C)	(D)
45.	19543 Business Circle	(A)	(B)	(C)	(D)
46.	1517 Grinnell Drive	(A)	(B)	(C)	(D)
47.	87 Rural Route 2	(A)	(B)	(C)	(D)
48.	201 W 63rd St	(A)	(B)	(C)	(D)
49.	2197 Greystone Pl	(A)	(B)	(C)	(D)
50.	623 Forest Lawn	(A)	(B)	(C)	(D)
51.	1234 Andalusia Way	(A)	(B)	(C)	(D)
52.	134 Rural Route 2	(A)	(B)	(C)	(D)
53.	1422 Grinnell Drive	(A)	(B)	(C)	(D)
54.	310 W 63rd St	(A)	(B)	(C)	(D)
55.	301 Forest Lawn	(A)	(B)	(C)	(D)
56.	19877 Business Circle	(A)	(B)	(C)	(D)

57.	882 Forest Lawn	Ⓐ	Ⓑ	Ⓒ	Ⓓ
58.	555 S Pittsdale Hwy	Ⓐ	Ⓑ	Ⓒ	Ⓓ
59.	2122 Greystone Pl	Ⓐ	Ⓑ	Ⓒ	Ⓓ
60.	143 Rural Route 2	Ⓐ	Ⓑ	Ⓒ	Ⓓ
61.	2020 Greystoke Pl	Ⓐ	Ⓑ	Ⓒ	Ⓓ
62.	1625 Grinnell Dr	Ⓐ	Ⓑ	Ⓒ	Ⓓ
63.	1151 Andalusia Way	Ⓐ	Ⓑ	Ⓒ	Ⓓ
64.	17601 Business Circle	Ⓐ	Ⓑ	Ⓒ	Ⓓ
65.	419 W 63rd St	Ⓐ	Ⓑ	Ⓒ	Ⓓ
66.	520 S Pittsdale Hwy	Ⓐ	Ⓑ	Ⓒ	Ⓓ
67.	2142 Greystone Pl	Ⓐ	Ⓑ	Ⓒ	Ⓓ
68.	11 Rural Route 2	Ⓐ	Ⓑ	Ⓒ	Ⓓ
69.	16606 Business Circle	Ⓐ	Ⓑ	Ⓒ	Ⓓ
70.	410 W 63rd St	Ⓐ	Ⓑ	Ⓒ	Ⓓ
71.	1689 Grinnell Dr	Ⓐ	Ⓑ	Ⓒ	Ⓓ
72.	2070 Greystone Pl	Ⓐ	Ⓑ	Ⓒ	Ⓓ

This is the end of Part C: Coding Section, Practice Test 4.

Part D: Personal Characteristics and Experience Inventory

As explained earlier, it is not possible to prepare for or practice the 236 job-related characteristics and experience questions in Part D. Therefore, no test items are included in this practice exam. For examples, please see Chapters 2 and 6.

Remember, there are no right or wrong answers in this section of Postal Test 473/473-C. Moreover, the USPS does not reveal how it evaluates the highly personal responses to Part D, nor how it weighs this part.

Feel confident that if you select the one response for each statement/question that best reflects your own personality, experience, and work ethics, you will be honestly representing yourself.

ANSWER KEY FOR PRACTICE TEST 4

Part A: Address Checking

1.	D	21.	C	41.	C
2.	C	22.	D	42.	D
3.	B	23.	C	43.	C
4.	B	24.	C	44.	A
5.	A	25.	A	45.	A
6.	C	26.	B	46.	B
7.	C	27.	B	47.	B
8.	B	28.	D	48.	C
9.	D	29.	C	49.	C
10.	A	30.	C	50.	D
11.	C	31.	C	51.	B
12.	C	32.	A	52.	C
13.	B	33.	C	53.	B
14.	A	34.	B	54.	A
15.	D	35.	C	55.	B
16.	C	36.	B	56.	C
17.	B	37.	B	57.	C
18.	B	38.	D	58.	B
19.	B	39.	A	59.	D
20.	A	40.	B	60.	A

Part B: Forms Completion

1.	D	11.	B	21.	A
2.	A	12.	A	22.	B
3.	D	13.	C	23.	C
4.	B	14.	D	24.	D
5.	A	15.	A	25.	D
6.	C	16.	A	26.	B
7.	A	17.	C	27.	C
8.	D	18.	B	28.	A
9.	C	19.	D	29.	C
10.	D	20.	C	30.	C

Part C: Coding and Memory

1.	A	25.	D	49.	D
2.	D	26.	B	50.	B
3.	A	27.	B	51.	A
4.	C	28.	C	52.	C
5.	C	29.	A	53.	A
6.	B	30.	C	54.	A
7.	B	31.	A	55.	D
8.	A	32.	D	56.	B
9.	C	33.	B	57.	B
10.	D	34.	D	58.	C
11.	C	35.	A	59.	C
12.	C	36.	C	60.	C
13.	A	37.	C	61.	D
14.	A	38.	C	62.	A
15.	A	39.	D	63.	A
16.	B	40.	A	64.	B
17.	D	41.	A	65.	A
18.	B	42.	B	66.	C
19.	C	43.	D	67.	C
20.	C	44.	B	68.	D
21.	B	45.	B	69.	B
22.	A	46.	A	70.	A
23.	D	47.	C	71.	A
24.	A	48.	A	72.	C

Postal Exam 473/473-C
Practice Test Answer Sheet

Tear out or photocopy one two-sided Answer Sheet for each Practice Test. This sheet is similar to the one you will mark at the real exam.

When taking the actual Test 473 or 473-C, you will first fill in the top half of the front side of the Answer Sheet, which asks for information similar to what you provided when applying for the exam. You will mark your answers for Address Checking and Forms Completion on the bottom half of the first side.

On the back side of the Answer Sheet, you will mark your answers for the final two sections of the test: Coding and Memory and Personal Characteristics and Experience Inventory.

For some excellent tips on marking your Answer Sheet, please see **Appendix A: Five Valuable Answer Sheet Marking Strategies** in the back of this book.

Part A: Address Checking

1 Ⓐ Ⓑ Ⓒ Ⓓ	11 Ⓐ Ⓑ Ⓒ Ⓓ	21 Ⓐ Ⓑ Ⓒ Ⓓ	31 Ⓐ Ⓑ Ⓒ Ⓓ	41 Ⓐ Ⓑ Ⓒ Ⓓ	51 Ⓐ Ⓑ Ⓒ Ⓓ
2 Ⓐ Ⓑ Ⓒ Ⓓ	12 Ⓐ Ⓑ Ⓒ Ⓓ	22 Ⓐ Ⓑ Ⓒ Ⓓ	32 Ⓐ Ⓑ Ⓒ Ⓓ	42 Ⓐ Ⓑ Ⓒ Ⓓ	52 Ⓐ Ⓑ Ⓒ Ⓓ
3 Ⓐ Ⓑ Ⓒ Ⓓ	13 Ⓐ Ⓑ Ⓒ Ⓓ	23 Ⓐ Ⓑ Ⓒ Ⓓ	33 Ⓐ Ⓑ Ⓒ Ⓓ	43 Ⓐ Ⓑ Ⓒ Ⓓ	53 Ⓐ Ⓑ Ⓒ Ⓓ
4 Ⓐ Ⓑ Ⓒ Ⓓ	14 Ⓐ Ⓑ Ⓒ Ⓓ	24 Ⓐ Ⓑ Ⓒ Ⓓ	34 Ⓐ Ⓑ Ⓒ Ⓓ	44 Ⓐ Ⓑ Ⓒ Ⓓ	54 Ⓐ Ⓑ Ⓒ Ⓓ
5 Ⓐ Ⓑ Ⓒ Ⓓ	15 Ⓐ Ⓑ Ⓒ Ⓓ	25 Ⓐ Ⓑ Ⓒ Ⓓ	35 Ⓐ Ⓑ Ⓒ Ⓓ	45 Ⓐ Ⓑ Ⓒ Ⓓ	55 Ⓐ Ⓑ Ⓒ Ⓓ
6 Ⓐ Ⓑ Ⓒ Ⓓ	16 Ⓐ Ⓑ Ⓒ Ⓓ	26 Ⓐ Ⓑ Ⓒ Ⓓ	36 Ⓐ Ⓑ Ⓒ Ⓓ	46 Ⓐ Ⓑ Ⓒ Ⓓ	56 Ⓐ Ⓑ Ⓒ Ⓓ
7 Ⓐ Ⓑ Ⓒ Ⓓ	17 Ⓐ Ⓑ Ⓒ Ⓓ	27 Ⓐ Ⓑ Ⓒ Ⓓ	37 Ⓐ Ⓑ Ⓒ Ⓓ	47 Ⓐ Ⓑ Ⓒ Ⓓ	57 Ⓐ Ⓑ Ⓒ Ⓓ
8 Ⓐ Ⓑ Ⓒ Ⓓ	18 Ⓐ Ⓑ Ⓒ Ⓓ	28 Ⓐ Ⓑ Ⓒ Ⓓ	38 Ⓐ Ⓑ Ⓒ Ⓓ	48 Ⓐ Ⓑ Ⓒ Ⓓ	58 Ⓐ Ⓑ Ⓒ Ⓓ
9 Ⓐ Ⓑ Ⓒ Ⓓ	19 Ⓐ Ⓑ Ⓒ Ⓓ	29 Ⓐ Ⓑ Ⓒ Ⓓ	39 Ⓐ Ⓑ Ⓒ Ⓓ	49 Ⓐ Ⓑ Ⓒ Ⓓ	59 Ⓐ Ⓑ Ⓒ Ⓓ
10 Ⓐ Ⓑ Ⓒ Ⓓ	20 Ⓐ Ⓑ Ⓒ Ⓓ	30 Ⓐ Ⓑ Ⓒ Ⓓ	40 Ⓐ Ⓑ Ⓒ Ⓓ	50 Ⓐ Ⓑ Ⓒ Ⓓ	60 Ⓐ Ⓑ Ⓒ Ⓓ

Part B: Forms Completion

1 Ⓐ Ⓑ Ⓒ Ⓓ	6 Ⓐ Ⓑ Ⓒ Ⓓ	11 Ⓐ Ⓑ Ⓒ Ⓓ	16 Ⓐ Ⓑ Ⓒ Ⓓ	21 Ⓐ Ⓑ Ⓒ Ⓓ	26 Ⓐ Ⓑ Ⓒ Ⓓ
2 Ⓐ Ⓑ Ⓒ Ⓓ	7 Ⓐ Ⓑ Ⓒ Ⓓ	12 Ⓐ Ⓑ Ⓒ Ⓓ	17 Ⓐ Ⓑ Ⓒ Ⓓ	22 Ⓐ Ⓑ Ⓒ Ⓓ	27 Ⓐ Ⓑ Ⓒ Ⓓ
3 Ⓐ Ⓑ Ⓒ Ⓓ	8 Ⓐ Ⓑ Ⓒ Ⓓ	13 Ⓐ Ⓑ Ⓒ Ⓓ	18 Ⓐ Ⓑ Ⓒ Ⓓ	23 Ⓐ Ⓑ Ⓒ Ⓓ	28 Ⓐ Ⓑ Ⓒ Ⓓ
4 Ⓐ Ⓑ Ⓒ Ⓓ	9 Ⓐ Ⓑ Ⓒ Ⓓ	14 Ⓐ Ⓑ Ⓒ Ⓓ	19 Ⓐ Ⓑ Ⓒ Ⓓ	24 Ⓐ Ⓑ Ⓒ Ⓓ	29 Ⓐ Ⓑ Ⓒ Ⓓ
5 Ⓐ Ⓑ Ⓒ Ⓓ	10 Ⓐ Ⓑ Ⓒ Ⓓ	15 Ⓐ Ⓑ Ⓒ Ⓓ	20 Ⓐ Ⓑ Ⓒ Ⓓ	25 Ⓐ Ⓑ Ⓒ Ⓓ	30 Ⓐ Ⓑ Ⓒ Ⓓ

continued on other side →

KAPLAN

Part C: Coding and Memory

Coding Section		Memory Section

Coding Section

1 (A) (B) (C) (D)   13 (A) (B) (C) (D)   25 (A) (B) (C) (D)
2 (A) (B) (C) (D)   14 (A) (B) (C) (D)   26 (A) (B) (C) (D)
3 (A) (B) (C) (D)   15 (A) (B) (C) (D)   27 (A) (B) (C) (D)
4 (A) (B) (C) (D)   16 (A) (B) (C) (D)   28 (A) (B) (C) (D)
5 (A) (B) (C) (D)   17 (A) (B) (C) (D)   29 (A) (B) (C) (D)
6 (A) (B) (C) (D)   18 (A) (B) (C) (D)   30 (A) (B) (C) (D)
7 (A) (B) (C) (D)   19 (A) (B) (C) (D)   31 (A) (B) (C) (D)
8 (A) (B) (C) (D)   20 (A) (B) (C) (D)   32 (A) (B) (C) (D)
9 (A) (B) (C) (D)   21 (A) (B) (C) (D)   33 (A) (B) (C) (D)
10 (A) (B) (C) (D)   22 (A) (B) (C) (D)   34 (A) (B) (C) (D)
11 (A) (B) (C) (D)   23 (A) (B) (C) (D)   35 (A) (B) (C) (D)
12 (A) (B) (C) (D)   24 (A) (B) (C) (D)   36 (A) (B) (C) (D)

Memory Section

37 (A) (B) (C) (D)   49 (A) (B) (C) (D)   61 (A) (B) (C) (D)
38 (A) (B) (C) (D)   50 (A) (B) (C) (D)   62 (A) (B) (C) (D)
39 (A) (B) (C) (D)   51 (A) (B) (C) (D)   63 (A) (B) (C) (D)
40 (A) (B) (C) (D)   52 (A) (B) (C) (D)   64 (A) (B) (C) (D)
41 (A) (B) (C) (D)   53 (A) (B) (C) (D)   65 (A) (B) (C) (D)
42 (A) (B) (C) (D)   54 (A) (B) (C) (D)   66 (A) (B) (C) (D)
43 (A) (B) (C) (D)   55 (A) (B) (C) (D)   67 (A) (B) (C) (D)
44 (A) (B) (C) (D)   56 (A) (B) (C) (D)   68 (A) (B) (C) (D)
45 (A) (B) (C) (D)   57 (A) (B) (C) (D)   69 (A) (B) (C) (D)
46 (A) (B) (C) (D)   58 (A) (B) (C) (D)   70 (A) (B) (C) (D)
47 (A) (B) (C) (D)   59 (A) (B) (C) (D)   71 (A) (B) (C) (D)
48 (A) (B) (C) (D)   60 (A) (B) (C) (D)   72 (A) (B) (C) (D)

Part D: Personal Characteristics and Experience Inventory

[When taking the real Test 473/473-C, you will mark the answers to the 236 questions in this area of the Answer Sheet.]

PRACTICE TEST 5

Part A: Address Checking

Instructions

Part A has 60 questions. You will have 11 minutes to complete this portion of the test. Each item (question) has two side-by-side addresses containing either identical or almost identical information.

You must compare each of the 60 items, decide if they are *exactly* the same or not, and mark the correct answers by blackening the corresponding ovals on your answer sheet. If the two addresses are different, you must decide if there is a difference in only the street address *or* in the ZIP code only *or* in both the street address *and* the ZIP code.

There are four answer choices, as you can see from the sample below; and the answer sheet has four ovals for each item, representing those four choices. If the two addresses are the same, darken oval A. If there is a difference in the street address only, darken oval B. If there is a difference in the ZIP code only, darken oval C. And if there is a difference in both the street address and the ZIP code, darken oval D.

A. No Errors   B. Address Only   C. ZIP Code Only   D. Both

Set your timer for exactly 11 minutes. Turn the page when you are ready and begin.

Part A: Address Checking

A. No Errors	B. Address Only	C. ZIP Code Only	D. Both

	Correct List		**List to Be Checked**	
	Address	**ZIP Code**	**Address**	**ZIP Code**
1.	2550 E Las Flores Ln Texarkana, AR	94501	2550 E Las Flores Ln Texarkana, AR	95501
2.	221½ Fox Hollow Pl Bridgeport, CT	65732	221½ Fox Hollow Pl Bridgeport, CT	65732
3.	21852 Inola Ave Atwater, CA	25817	21582 Inola Ave Atwater, CA	25187
4.	1668 Nicolle Dr Plantation, FL	27841	1668 Nicole Dr. Plantation, FL	27841
5.	901-B Storrs Pl Houma, LA	85628	901-D Storrs Pl Houma, LA	85628
6.	7724 Nielson Rd Longview, WA	25672	7724 Nielsen Rd. Longview, WA	25762
7.	60201 Enchilada Fairmont, WV	66209	60201 Enchilada Farmont, WV	66209
8.	22 W Blue Ridge Fire Rd Knoxville, TN	88346	22 W Blue Ridge Fire Rd Knoxville, TN	88346
9.	144 Corinth Ave Marshfield, WI	37109	144 Corinth Ave Marshfield, WI	37109
10.	166 W Lomita Blvd Hackensack, NJ	74937	166 W Lomita Blvd Hackensack, NJ	79437
11.	P.O. Box 12235 Buffalo, NY	50792	P.O. Box 12335 Buffalo, NY	50792
12.	6638 Pinetop Rd Tuskegee, AL	62837	6638 Pinetop Rd Tuskegee, AL	62387
13.	442 Rural Route 11 Owensboro, KY	91219	442 Rural Route 11 Owensboro, KY	92129
14.	1171 Garfield Ave Jefferson City, MO	15386	1171 Garfield Ave Jefferson City, MO	15836
15.	3178-D Divorce Ct Laughlin, NV	31775	3718 Divorce Ct Laughlin, NV	31775
16.	2510 Hesperia Ln Cheyenne, WY	33772	2510 Hesparia Ln Cheyenne, WY	37732

A. No Errors   B. Address Only   C. ZIP Code Only   D. Both

Correct List		**List to Be Checked**	
Address	**ZIP Code**	**Address**	**ZIP Code**
17. 2555 24th Ave SW Apple Valley, CA	82749	2555 24th Ave NW Apple Valley, CA	82149
18. 18811 W Hawk Ln Bar Harbor, ME	72157	18111 W Hawk Ln Bar Harbor, ME	72157
19. 19957 Suana Ter Tulsa, OK	25350	19957 Suana Ter Tulsa, OK	25350
20. 225 18th St SE Silver Spring, MD	99271	225 18th St SE Silver Spring, MD	99271
21. 146-A 155th Ave W Nogales, AZ	15782	146-A 155th Ave W Nogales, AZ	17582
22. 22591 Zelzah Fire Rd Sioux City, IA	74203	22591 Zelzah Fire Rd Sioux City, IA	74023
23. 135-F Faculty Dr New Haven, CT	57930	153-F Faculty Dr New Haven, CT	57390
24. 233 Alderwood Ln Sylacauga, AL	32951	233 Alderwood Ln Sylacauga, AL	32951
25. 21978 46th Ave NE Tallahassee, FL	42972	21978 46th Ave NE Tallahassee, FL	49272
26. 4422 Gas Line Rd Jackson, WY	47792	4422 Gas Line Rd Jackson, WY	47792
27. 28967 Ave B Bristol, RI	99678	28697 Ave B Bristol, RI	99678
28. 378-B Barbacoa Circle Sugar Land, TX	28274	378-B Barbacoa Circle Sugar Land, TX	28474
29. 225 Lochgreene Ln New Bedford, MA	95782	225 Lochgreene Ln New Bedford, MA	95872
30. 1739 Santa Mariana Ave Natchitoches, LA	17983	1789 Santa Mariana Ave Natchitoches, LA	19783
31. 1224 176th St NE Abilene, KS	78293	1224 179th St NE Abilene, KS	79283
32. 44761 Altura Dr Fort Wayne, IN	72681	44761 Altura Dr Fort Wayne, IN	72681
33. 22391 Corporate Point Fairfax, VA	10302-1776	22931 Corporate Point Fairfax, VA	10302-1776
34. 2278 Jefferson Lane Normal, IL	90205	2278 Jeffersen Lane Normal, IL	90205

A. No Errors	B. Address Only	C. ZIP Code Only	D. Both

Correct List		**List to Be Checked**	
Address	**ZIP Code**	**Address**	**ZIP Code**
35. P.O. Box 22992 Nenana, AK	22789	P.O. Box 29922 Nenana, AK	22789
36. 221-C Personnel Rd Kalamazoo, MI	27819	221-C Personnel Rd Kalamazoo, MI	27819
37. 226 Percheron Trace Hattiesburg, MS	19703	266 Percheron Trace Hattiesburg, MS	16703
38. 90392 Smiley Drive Somersworth, NH	14927	90092 Smiley Drive Somersworth, NH	14297
39. 227 Preciado Pl Gallup, NM	24693	227 Preciado Pl Gallup, NM	24963
40. 1955 Converse Way Bandon, OR	62093	1955 Converse Way Bandon, OR	62093
41. P.O. Box 92810 State College, PA	21795-2438	P.O. Box 98210 State College, PA	21795-2438
42. 22 Cow Creek Court Pulaski, TN	62783	22 Cow Creek Court Pulaski, TN	62873
43. 1382 Rancho Sinaloa Pl West Jordan, UT	92704	1382 Rancho Sineloa Pl West Jordan, UT	92704
44. 163 Quailhill Dr Cheney, WV	57928	193 Quailhill Dr Cheney, WV	59728
45. 2851 Norlina Blvd Seattle, WA	62891	2581 Norlina Blvd Seattle, WA	62891
46. 29-C Interception Ave Langley, VA	79281	29-C Interception Ave Langley, VA	79281
47. 33 Jackrabbit Run Bozeman, MT	28719	33 Jackrabbit Run Bozeman, MT	27819
48. 21-D Eddingham Way Henderson, NV	42063	21-D Eddingham Way Henderson, NV	42603
49. 633 S Eastern Ave Cape Girardeau, MO	42404	633 S Western Ave Cape Girardeau, MO	42404
50. 44 Brass Lantern Dr Kalama, WA	92601	44 Brass Lantern Dr Kalama, WA	92601
51. 6279½ W Lime Ave Wahoo, NE	14897	6279¼ W Lime Ave Wahoo, NE	14987
52. 1677 W 42nd Ave S Williston, ND	24976-9742	1667 W 42nd Ave S Williston, ND	24976-6742

| A. No Errors | B. Address Only | C. ZIP Code Only | D. Both |

Correct List		**List to Be Checked**	
Address	**ZIP Code**	**Address**	**ZIP Code**
53. 6789 Girard Ter Kenosha, WI	35701	6789 Girard Ter Kenosha, WI	37501
54. 1891 W Falcon Ave Vergennes, VT	95076	1981 W Falcon Ave Vergennes, VT	95076
55. 1633 Nearwood Pl Orangeburg, SC	68201	1633 Neerwood Pl Orangeburg, SC	68201
56. 4719 Sacramento Mysecret, ID	66204	4719 Sacramento Mysecret, ID	66204
57. 21 ¼ Sawtooth Ct Hamilton, OH	21604	21 ¼ Sawtooth Ct Hamilton, OH	26104
58. 8992 Via Codo Cary, NC	77291	8992 Via Godo Cary, NC	77291
59. 3271 Eddystone St Niagara Falls, NY	45801-4382	3271 Eddystone St Niagara Falls, NY	45081-4382
60. 12903 Loveland Eden Prairie, MN	62791	12903 Loveland Eden Prairie, MN	62791

This is the end of Part A: Address Checking Section, Practice Test 5.

Part B: Forms Completion

Part B consists of 30 questions that test your ability to identify the information needed to correctly complete various U.S. Postal Service forms. You will be shown 5 different forms, each followed by 6 questions.

Set your timer for exactly 15 minutes. Turn the page and begin when you are ready.

Part B: Forms Completion

Domestic Claim or Registered Mail Inquiry

Mailer Information	Addressee Information
1a. Name:	2a. Name:
1b. Business or Company Name:	2b. Business or Company Name:
1c. No. and Street, Apt/Suite:	2c. No. and Street, Apt/Suite:
1d. City, State, ZIP + 4:	2d. City, State, ZIP + 4:
1e. Telephone *(with area code):*	2e. Telephone *(with area code):*

3. Payment Assignment	4. Description of Lost or Damaged Article(s) (Add Extra Sheets as Needed)			
3a. Who is to receive payment? *(Check one)*	Item	Description	Purchase Date	Value
☐ Mailer	A	4a.		
☐ Addressee	B	4b.		
	C	4c.		
5a. COD Amount to be remitted to sender: $ _____	5b. Total amount claimed for all articles: $ _____			

Certification and Signature		
6a. Customer submitting claim: ☐ Mailer ☐ Addressee	6b. Customer Signature:	6c. Date Signed:

Part B: Forms Completion

1. For which of these would a dollar amount be an appropriate entry?
   A. Box 2a
   B. Box 5b
   C. Boxes 5a and 5b
   D. All of the above

2. The addressee is Dr. Susan Locke. Where would you indicate this?
   A. Box 1a
   B. Box 1b
   C. Box 2a
   D. Box 6b

3. Which of the following would be an acceptable entry for Box 3a?
   A. Larry Getz
   B. $96.40
   C. Salem, IL
   D. A check mark

4. Which of the following is a correct entry for Box 6b?
   A. A signature
   B. A check mark
   C. A date
   D. A postmark

5. On this form, three items are being claimed. Item A has a value of $100; Item B has a value of $65; and Item C has a value of $20. The total amount claimed is $185. Where should $185 be entered?
   A. Box 4a
   B. Box 5a
   C. Box 5b
   D. Box 6a

6. On this form, three items are being claimed. Item A has a value of $100; Item B has a value of $65; and Item C has a value of $20. The total amount claimed is $185. What should be entered in Box 5a?
   A. $100
   B. $20
   C. $185
   D. None of these

Part B: Forms Completion

Mail Forwarding Change of Address Order

		OFFICIAL USE ONLY
Please PRINT Items 1–10 in blue or black ink. Your signature is required in Item 9.		Zone/Route ID No.
1. Change of Address for: (Read Attached Inastructions) ☐ Individual (#5) ☐ Entire Family (#5) ☐ Business (#6)	2. Is This Move Temporary? ☐ Yes ☐ No	Date Entered on Form 3982 M M D D Y Y
3. Start Date:	4. If TEMPORARY move, print date to discontinue forwarding:	Expiration Date M M D D Y Y
5. LAST Name & Jr./Sr./etc.		Clerk/Carrier Endorsement
5b. FIRST Name and MI		
6. If BUSINESS Move, Print Business Name		

PRINT OLD MAILING ADDRESS BELOW: HOUSE/BUILDING NUMBER AND STREET NAME (INCLUDE ST., AVE., CT., ETC.) OR P.O. BOX			
7a. OLD Mailing Address			
7a. OLD APT or Suite	7b. For Puerto Rico Only: If address is in PR, print urbanization name, if appropriate		
7c. OLD CITY		7d. State	7e. ZIP
8a. NEW Mailing Address	8b. For Puerto Rico Only: If address is in PR, print urbanization name, if appropriate		
8c. NEW CITY		8d. State	8e. ZIP
9. Print and Sign Name (see conditions on reverse) ➤ Print: Sign:	10. Date Signed:		

Part B: Forms Completion

7. The old address is 820 Western Avenue. Where would this be entered?
   A. In the boxes in Line 6
   B. In the boxes in Line 7a
   C. In the boxes in Line 7b
   D. In the boxes in Line 8a

8. Which of these is an acceptable entry for Box 10?
   A. 11/27/07
   B. A check mark
   C. Robbie Healy
   D. WV

9. Which box is only for use with Puerto Rican addresses?
   A. Box 7b
   B. Box 7a and Box 8a
   C. Box 7b and Box 8b
   D. Boxes 7b, 8b, and 9

10. What is needed in the "Official Use Only" box?
    A. Clerk/Carrier Endorsement
    B. Expiration Date
    C. Zone/Route ID No.
    D. All of the above

11. How would the customer indicate that the move is temporary?
    A. A signature in Box 9
    B. A check mark next to "Yes" in Box 1
    C. A check mark next to "Yes" in Box 2
    D. A check mark next to "No" in Box 2

12. What colors of ink are acceptable to fill out this form?
    A. Black only
    B. Black or blue only
    C. Blue or green only
    D. Any color is acceptable

Part B: Forms Completion

Global Direct Notification of Mailing

A. General

1. Mailer's Name	2. Mailer's Address *(No., street, ste. no., city, state, ZIP + 4)*
3. Contact Person	
4a. Telephone No. *(Include area code)*	
4b. Fax No. *(Include area code)*	

5. Destination Country	6. Date Notified	7. Global Direct Customer ID No.

B. Mailing Information

8. Mailing Date	9. Estimated Total Mailing Weight	10. Container Quantity	11. Acceptance Location
		Trays _____ Pallets _____	☐ Plant-Verification Drop Shipment Location: ☐ Global Direct Acceptance Location:

12. Return Address *(See PS Form 3681 including Global Direct Customer Identification Number.)* Check the appropriate box:

☐ I will use my own in-country return address

☐ I will use the following USPS-provided in-country return address:

13. I am requesting the return of "Undeliverable-As-Addressed" items to the USPS in-country return address. I would like these items sent to the following US address *(No., street, ste. no., city, state, ZIP + 4)*:

NOTE: General correspondence and other items may occasionally be sent to this address by customers in the destination country. I agree to pay the USPS for the return of such items to my designated US address. For rate information, see the *IMM* and USPS publications on Global Direct Service.

C. Comments

Part B: Forms Completion

13. Which of these would be an acceptable entry for Box 5?
   A. South Dakota
   B. Wales
   C. Paris, France
   D. None of the above

14. The contact person is Gia Kyle. Where should this piece of information be entered?
   A. Box 1
   B. Box 2
   C. Box 3
   D. Box 13

15. Where would you write comments on this form?
   A. Anywhere in Section A
   B. Anywhere in Section B
   C. In Box 13 only
   D. Anywhere in Section C

16. Where would "909-555-6682" be an acceptable entry?
   A. Box 3
   B. Box 4a
   C. Box 4b
   D. Either 4a or 4b

17. Where would you indicate the acceptance location?
   A. Box 11
   B. Box 12
   C. Box 13
   D. Section C, "Comments"

18. Which of the following would be an appropriate entry for Box 6?
   A. $59.51
   B. October 21, 2007
   C. 354 Elmwood Drive
   D. Perishable

Part B: Forms Completion

Postage Statement - Special Services

<table>
<tr><td rowspan="8" style="writing-mode:vertical-lr">Mailer Info.</td><td>Permit Holder's Name, Address, and Email Address, If Any</td><td>Telephone</td><td colspan="2">Post Office of Mailing</td><td colspan="2">Form Number of Attached Postage Statement</td></tr>
<tr><td rowspan="7"></td><td rowspan="3">Mailing Date</td><td colspan="2" rowspan="3"></td><td>For Domestic</td><td>For International</td></tr>
<tr><td>☐ First-Class Mail</td><td>☐ Letter Post (LP)</td></tr>
<tr><td>☐ Priority Mail</td><td>☐ Parcel Post (PP)</td></tr>
<tr><td rowspan="2">Permit Number</td><td colspan="2" rowspan="2"></td><td>☐ Standard Mail</td><td>☐ Express Mail (EMS)</td></tr>
<tr><td rowspan="3">☐ Package Services</td><td rowspan="3"></td></tr>
<tr><td rowspan="2">Statement Sequence No.</td><td colspan="2" rowspan="2"></td></tr>
</table>

■ Domestic Mail

		Service	DMM Section	Number Pcs. x	Fee	Totals
	A1	Certificate of Mailing *(Three or more)*	S914		$ 0.30	
	A2	Certified Mail	S912		$ 2.30	
	A3	Collect on Delivery (COD)	S921			
	A4	Delivery Confirmation	S918			
	A5	Insured Mail	S913			
	A6	Registered Mail	S911			
	A7	Restricted Delivery	S916		$ 3.50	
	A8	Return Receipt	S915		$ 1.75	
	A9	*Reserved*				
	A10	Return Receipt for Merchandise	S917		$ 3.00	
	A11	Signature Confirmation	S919			
	A12	Parcel Airlift (PAL)	S930			
	A13	Special Handling	S930			
		Total Supplemental Postage *(Carry this amount to attached postage statement)* ➔				

■ International Mail

		Service	IMM Section	Number Pcs. x	Fee	Totals
	B1	Insurance	320			
	B2	Recorded Delivery	360		$ 2.30	
	B3	Registered Mail	330			
	B4	Restricted Delivery	350		$ 3.50	
	B5	Return Receipt	340		$ 1.75	
		Total Supplemental Postage *(Carry this amount to attached PS Form 3651)* ➔				

Part B: Forms Completion

19. There are 45 pieces for Recorded Delivery service. What is the fee per piece?
   A. $2.30
   B. $3.00
   C. $3.50
   D. None of the above

20. In which row would you insert information about Signature Confirmation?
   A. Row A2
   B. Row A9
   C. Row A11
   D. Row B3

21. In which row would you insert information about Registered Mail?
   A. Row A6
   B. Row A10
   C. Row A6 and Row B2
   D. Row A6 and Row B3

22. Where should the permit number be entered?
   A. In the Mailer Info. section
   B. In the Domestic Mail section
   C. In the International Mail section
   D. Next to "Total Supplemental Postage"

23. What is PAL an abbreviation for?
   A. Parcel Air Luggage
   B. Parcel Airlift
   C. Priority Airmail Letters
   D. None of the above

24. Which service is represented in Row A4?
   A. Domestic Certified Mail
   B. Domestic Insured Mail
   C. Domestic Recorded Delivery
   D. None of the above

Part B: Forms Completion

Return Receipt for International Mail

<table>
<tr>
<td rowspan="7">Completed by office of origin</td>
<td colspan="3"></td>
</tr>
<tr>
<td colspan="3">1. Item Description:
☐ Registered Article   ☐ Letter   ☐ Printed Matter   ☐ Other</td>
</tr>
<tr>
<td>2a. ☐ Insured Parcel</td>
<td>2b. Insured Value</td>
<td>2c. Article Number</td>
</tr>
<tr>
<td colspan="2">3a. Office of Mailing</td>
<td>3b. Date of Posting</td>
</tr>
<tr>
<td colspan="3">4. Addressee Name or Firm</td>
</tr>
<tr>
<td colspan="3">5. Street and No.</td>
</tr>
<tr>
<td colspan="3">6. Place and Country</td>
</tr>
<tr>
<td rowspan="3">Completed at destination</td>
<td colspan="2">7. Postmark of the Office of Destination</td>
<td>8. ☐ The article mentioned above was duly delivered.</td>
</tr>
<tr>
<td colspan="2">9a. Signature of Addressee</td>
<td>9b. Date</td>
</tr>
<tr>
<td colspan="3">10. Office of Destination Employee Signature</td>
</tr>
</table>

Part B: Forms Completion

25. Which of the following would be an appropriate entry for Box 4?
- A. The Cactus Card Company
- B. Chicago, IL 45893-5312
- C. 11/02/06
- D. 10 Macon Lane

26. Which of the following would be an appropriate entry for Box 5?
- A. The Cactus Card Company
- B. Chicago, IL 45893-5312
- C. 11/02/06
- D. 10 Macon Lane

27. Which of the following would be an appropriate entry for Box 9b?
- A. The Cactus Card Company
- B. Chicago, IL 45893-5312
- C. 11/02/06
- D. 10 Macon Lane

28. Where should the addressee's signature be entered?
- A. Box 7
- B. Box 9a
- C. Box 10
- D. The addressee's signature is not requested on this form.

29. In which of the following would "Canada" be correctly entered?
- A. Box 3a
- B. Box 5
- C. Box 6
- D. Box 7

30. For which of these would the entry "$250" be acceptable?
- A. Box 1
- B. Box 2a
- C. Box 2b
- D. Box 2b and Box 2c

This is the end of Part B: Forms Completion, Practice Test 5.

Part C: Coding and Memory

Overview

In Part C you will need to work quickly and accurately, using one Coding Guide to answer questions in two separate sections, the Coding Section and the Memory Section.

Prior to the scored segments of both the Coding Section and the Memory Section, there are practice segments. This test will follow the same format.

The Coding Guide that is used throughout Part C consists of four delivery routes. Three of the routes have two or three address ranges associated with them, and the last route covers any address not within the other three routes.

Each question (item) in both the Coding Section and the Memory Section consists of an address. Your job is to determine which of the four routes a given address belongs to and to mark your answer sheet accordingly.

In the Coding Section you may use the Coding Guide to determine the correct route for each address. In the Memory Section you will see exactly the same type of questions that are in the Coding Section, but you will no longer be able to look at the Coding Guide. Rather, you must determine which of the four routes an address belongs to, using only your memory of the Coding Guide.

The scored portion of the Coding Section has 36 questions, and you have 6 minutes to answer them. Prior to the scored portion, you will have two opportunities to practice using the Coding Guide.

The scored portion of the Memory Section also has 36 questions and 7 minutes to answer them. It also provides you with two opportunities to study and memorize the Coding Guide, as well as a chance to practice answering questions without using the Coding Guide.

Part C: Coding Section

Part 1: Sample Questions

Instructions   Answering the questions on the following pages will familiarize you with the format and timing of the questions in Part C: Coding Section. You will have 3½ minutes to answer 12 questions, using the Coding Guide displayed opposite the questions.

Mark your answers in the sample ovals and check your answers using the correct answers shown at the bottom of the same page.

Set your timer for 3½ minutes and turn the page when you are ready to begin.

Part C: Coding Section

Coding Guide	
Address Range	**Delivery Route**
779–2214 Lysander Dr 261–785 E 44th St 1100–1990 Finley Ave	A
1630–2301 W Olive 22090–30020 Clinton Pkwy	B
1956–2500 Griffith Park 250–700 E Rockland Hwy 99–215 Rural Route 5	C
Any mail that is not found in one of the above address ranges	D

Part C: Coding Section

Exercise 1: Sample Questions

	Address	Delivery Route			
1.	695 E Rockland Hwy	(A)	(B)	(C)	(D)
2.	1470 Finley Ave	(A)	(B)	(C)	(D)
3.	2110 Lysander Dr	(A)	(B)	(C)	(D)
4.	2002 W Olive	(A)	(B)	(C)	(D)
5.	796 E 44th St	(A)	(B)	(C)	(D)
6.	2450 Griffith Park	(A)	(B)	(C)	(D)
7.	110 Rural Route 5	(A)	(B)	(C)	(D)
8.	1870 Finley Ave	(A)	(B)	(C)	(D)
9.	781 Lysander Dr	(A)	(B)	(C)	(D)
10.	2100 W Olive	(A)	(B)	(C)	(D)
11.	225 E Rockland Hwy	(A)	(B)	(C)	(D)
12.	29010 Clinton Pkwy	(A)	(B)	(C)	(D)

Answers

1. C
2. A
3. A
4. B
5. D
6. C
7. C
8. A
9. A
10. B
11. D
12. B

Part C: Coding Section

Coding Practice Test 5

Instructions   This section follows the format of Postal Exam 473. There are 36 questions, and you will have 6 minutes to answer them. Each page of questions is displayed opposite the Coding Guide, which you may use to answer the questions.

You will score this section and use it to help determine your score on this practice test. Mark your answers on your Practice Test 5 Answer Sheet in the Coding Section of Part C.

Set your timer for 6 minutes and turn the page when you are ready to begin.

Coding Guide	
Address Range	**Delivery Route**
779–2214 Lysander Dr 261–785 E 44th St 1100–1990 Finley Ave	A
1630–2301 W Olive 22090–30020 Clinton Pkwy	B
1956–2500 Griffith Park 250–700 E Rockland Hwy 99–215 Rural Route 5	C
Any mail that is not found in one of the above address ranges	D

Coding Section: Practice Test 5

Questions

	Address	Delivery Route			
1.	2211 Lysander Dr	(A)	(B)	(C)	(D)
2.	161 E 44th St	(A)	(B)	(C)	(D)
3.	1999 Griffith Park	(A)	(B)	(C)	(D)
4.	115 Rural Route 5	(A)	(B)	(C)	(D)
5.	1760 W Olive	(A)	(B)	(C)	(D)
6.	1112 Finley Ave	(A)	(B)	(C)	(D)
7.	30012 Clinton Pkwy	(A)	(B)	(C)	(D)
8.	620 E Rockland Hwy	(A)	(B)	(C)	(D)
9.	101 Rural Route 5	(A)	(B)	(C)	(D)
10.	2318 Griffith Park	(A)	(B)	(C)	(D)
11.	1830 W Olvera	(A)	(B)	(C)	(D)
12.	277 E 44th St	(A)	(B)	(C)	(D)
13.	791 Lysander Dr	(A)	(B)	(C)	(D)
14.	695 W Rockland Hwy	(A)	(B)	(C)	(D)
15.	1985 Finley Ave	(A)	(B)	(C)	(D)
16.	22691 Clinton Pkwy	(A)	(B)	(C)	(D)
17.	210 Rural Route 5	(A)	(B)	(C)	(D)
18.	27504 Clinton Pkwy	(A)	(B)	(C)	(D)
19.	1866 W Olive	(A)	(B)	(C)	(D)
20.	261 E 44th Ave	(A)	(B)	(C)	(D)

Coding Guide	
Address Range	**Delivery Route**
779–2214 Lysander Dr 261–785 E 44th St 1100–1990 Finley Ave	A
1630–2301 W Olive 22090–30020 Clinton Pkwy	B
1956–2500 Griffith Park 250–700 E Rockland Hwy 99–215 Rural Route 5	C
Any mail that is not found in one of the above address ranges	D

21.	2090 Clinton Pkwy	A	B	C	D
22.	277 E Rockland Hwy	A	B	C	D
23.	2110 Lysander Dr	A	B	C	D
24.	2175 Griffith Park	A	B	C	D
25.	667 E Rockland Hwy	A	B	C	D
26.	185 Rural Route 3	A	B	C	D
27.	1692 W Olive	A	B	C	D
28.	1331 Finley Ave	A	B	C	D
29.	1683 Griffith Park	A	B	C	D
30.	24597 Clinton Pkwy	A	B	C	D
31.	2020 Lysander Dr	A	B	C	D
32.	1550 Finley Ave	A	B	C	D
33.	682 E 44th St	A	B	C	D
34.	179 Rural Route 5	A	B	C	D
35.	342 E Rockland Hwy	A	B	C	D
36.	1000 Finley Ave	A	B	C	D

This is the end of Part C: Coding Section, Practice Test 5.

Part C: Memory Section

Overview

There are four divisions in Part C: Memory Section. They are

1. a 3-minute period for studying the Coding Guide;
2. a 90-second nonscored practice, in which you answer 8 questions without using the Coding Guide;
3. a 5-minute period for studying the Coding Guide; and
4. a scored test, consisting of 36 questions, timed for 7 minutes.

During the two study periods there are no questions to answer; you are memorizing the Coding Guide. Section 2 is a timed practice test, with 8 questions to answer in 90 seconds, and a sample answer sheet. Section 4 is the actual test. Use the Practice Test 5 answer sheet to mark your answers. They will be scored.

Memory Section: Part 1

Instructions

Part 1 of the Memory Section is a study period. Use it to memorize the Coding Guide. There are no questions to answer during the 3-minute study period.

Set your timer for 3 minutes, and when you are ready to begin, turn the page.

Memory Section: Part 1

Coding Guide	
Address Range	**Delivery Route**
779–2214 Lysander Dr 261–785 E 44th St 1100–1990 Finley Ave	A
1630–2301 W Olive 22090–30020 Clinton Pkwy	B
1956–2500 Griffith Park 250–700 E Rockland Hwy 99–215 Rural Route 5	C
Any mail that is not found in one of the Above address ranges	D

Memory Section: Part 2

Instructions

In Part 2 of the Memory Section you will practice answering questions using your memory of the Coding Guide (see p. 241), which will not be shown. This is only a practice exercise; it will not be scored.

Following the eight questions is a sample answer sheet that you will use to mark your answers. At the bottom of the page is the answer key for the sample questions.

Set your timer for 90 seconds; when you are ready, you may begin.

Memory Section: Part 2

	Address	Delivery Route			
1.	99 Rural Route 5	(A)	(B)	(C)	(D)
2.	1360 W Olive	(A)	(B)	(C)	(D)
3.	1684 Finley Ave	(A)	(B)	(C)	(D)
4.	1097 Lysander Dr	(A)	(B)	(C)	(D)
5.	610 E Rockland Hwy	(A)	(B)	(C)	(D)
6.	1844 W Olive	(A)	(B)	(C)	(D)
7.	30012 Clinton Pkwy	(A)	(B)	(C)	(D)
8.	1988 Griffith Park	(A)	(B)	(C)	(D)

Answers

1. C
2. D
3. A
4. A
5. C
6. B
7. B
8. C

Memory Section: Part 3

Instructions

Part 3 of the Memory Section is a 5-minute study period. This is your final preparation period for the scored Memory test. Use it to finish memorizing the Coding Guide. As in Part 1 of this section, there are no questions to answer. Do not make marks of any kind during this study period.

Set your timer for 5 minutes, and when you are ready, turn the page and begin.

Memory Section: Part 3

Coding Guide	
Address Range	**Delivery Route**
779–2214 Lysander Dr 261–785 E 44th St 1100–1990 Finley Ave	A
1630–2301 W Olive 22090–30020 Clinton Pkwy	B
1956–2500 Griffith Park 250–700 E Rockland Hwy 99–215 Rural Route 5	C
Any mail that is not found in one of the above address ranges	D

Memory Section: Part 4

Instructions

Part 4 of the Memory Section is the scored Memory test. You will have 7 minutes to answer the 36 questions, without using the Coding Guide. You must answer the questions from memory.

Mark your answers to these 36 questions on the Practice Test 5 Answer Sheet, using lines 37–72 of Part C: Coding and Memory. When you have finished, it is time to score the exam.

Set your timer for 7 minutes, and when you are ready, begin.

Memory Section: Practice Test 5

Questions

	Address	Delivery Route			
37.	66 Rural Route 5	Ⓐ	Ⓑ	Ⓒ	Ⓓ
38.	1881 Finley Ave	Ⓐ	Ⓑ	Ⓒ	Ⓓ
39.	2091 Lysander Dr	Ⓐ	Ⓑ	Ⓒ	Ⓓ
40.	360 E 44th St	Ⓐ	Ⓑ	Ⓒ	Ⓓ
41.	2401 Griffith Park	Ⓐ	Ⓑ	Ⓒ	Ⓓ
42.	29902 Clinton Pkwy	Ⓐ	Ⓑ	Ⓒ	Ⓓ
43.	206 Rural Route 5	Ⓐ	Ⓑ	Ⓒ	Ⓓ
44.	1959 Griffith Park	Ⓐ	Ⓑ	Ⓒ	Ⓓ
45.	1370 Finely Ave	Ⓐ	Ⓑ	Ⓒ	Ⓓ
46.	29906 Clinton Pkwy	Ⓐ	Ⓑ	Ⓒ	Ⓓ
47.	1920 W Olive	Ⓐ	Ⓑ	Ⓒ	Ⓓ
48.	780 Lysander Dr	Ⓐ	Ⓑ	Ⓒ	Ⓓ
49.	187 Rural Route 5	Ⓐ	Ⓑ	Ⓒ	Ⓓ
50.	517 E Rockland Hwy	Ⓐ	Ⓑ	Ⓒ	Ⓓ
51.	29500 Clinten Pkwy	Ⓐ	Ⓑ	Ⓒ	Ⓓ
52.	2300 W Olive	Ⓐ	Ⓑ	Ⓒ	Ⓓ
53.	678 E 44th St	Ⓐ	Ⓑ	Ⓒ	Ⓓ
54.	1989 Finley Ave	Ⓐ	Ⓑ	Ⓒ	Ⓓ
55.	213 Rural Route 5	Ⓐ	Ⓑ	Ⓒ	Ⓓ
56.	451 E Rockland Hwy	Ⓐ	Ⓑ	Ⓒ	Ⓓ

57.	1982 Lysander Pl	(A)	(B)	(C)	(D)
58.	2398 Griffith Park	(A)	(B)	(C)	(D)
59.	22099 Clinton Pkwy	(A)	(B)	(C)	(D)
60.	1158 Finley Ave	(A)	(B)	(C)	(D)
61.	2201 S Olive	(A)	(B)	(C)	(D)
62.	2510 Griffith Park	(A)	(B)	(C)	(D)
63.	2115 Lysander Dr	(A)	(B)	(C)	(D)
64.	682 E Rockland Hwy	(A)	(B)	(C)	(D)
65.	205 Rural Route 5	(A)	(B)	(C)	(D)
66.	30001 Clinton Pkwy	(A)	(B)	(C)	(D)
67.	686 E 44th St	(A)	(B)	(C)	(D)
68.	1639 W Olive	(A)	(B)	(C)	(D)
69.	1925 Lysander Dr	(A)	(B)	(C)	(D)
70.	193 Rural Route 5	(A)	(B)	(C)	(D)
71.	1995 Finley Ave	(A)	(B)	(C)	(D)
72.	699 E Rockland Hwy	(A)	(B)	(C)	(D)

This is the end of Part C: Memory Section, Practice Test 5.

Part D: Personal Characteristics and Experience Inventory

As explained earlier, it is not possible to prepare for or practice the 236 job-related characteristics and experience questions in Part D. Therefore, no test items are included in this practice exam. For examples, please see Chapters 2 and 6.

Remember, there are no right or wrong answers in this section of Postal Test 473/473-C. Moreover, the USPS does not reveal how it evaluates the highly personal responses to Part D, nor how it weighs this part.

Feel confident that if you select the one response for each statement/question that best reflects your own personality, experience, and work ethics, you will be honestly representing yourself.

ANSWER KEY FOR PRACTICE TEST 5

Part A: Address Checking

1.	C	**21.**	C	**41.**	B
2.	A	**22.**	C	**42.**	C
3.	D	**23.**	D	**43.**	B
4.	B	**24.**	A	**44.**	D
5.	B	**25.**	C	**45.**	B
6.	D	**26.**	A	**46.**	A
7.	B	**27.**	B	**47.**	C
8.	A	**28.**	C	**48.**	C
9.	A	**29.**	C	**49.**	B
10.	C	**30.**	D	**50.**	A
11.	B	**31.**	D	**51.**	D
12.	C	**32.**	A	**52.**	D
13.	C	**33.**	B	**53.**	C
14.	C	**34.**	B	**54.**	B
15.	B	**35.**	B	**55.**	B
16.	D	**36.**	A	**56.**	A
17.	D	**37.**	D	**57.**	C
18.	B	**38.**	D	**58.**	B
19.	A	**39.**	C	**59.**	C
20.	A	**40.**	A	**60.**	A

KAPLAN

Part B: Forms Completion

1.	C	11.	C	21.	D
2.	C	12.	B	22.	A
3.	D	13.	B	23.	B
4.	A	14.	C	24.	D
5.	C	15.	D	25.	A
6.	D	16.	D	26.	D
7.	B	17.	A	27.	C
8.	A	18.	B	28.	B
9.	C	19.	A	29.	C
10.	D	20.	C	30.	C

Part C: Coding and Memory

1.	A	25.	C	49.	C
2.	D	26.	D	50.	C
3.	C	27.	B	51.	D
4.	C	28.	A	52.	B
5.	B	29.	D	53.	A
6.	A	30.	B	54.	A
7.	B	31.	A	55.	C
8.	C	32.	A	56.	C
9.	C	33.	A	57.	D
10.	C	34.	C	58.	C
11.	D	35.	C	59.	B
12.	A	36.	D	60.	A
13.	A	37.	D	61.	D
14.	D	38.	A	62.	D
15.	A	39.	A	63.	A
16.	B	40.	A	64.	C
17.	C	41.	C	65.	C
18.	B	42.	B	66.	B
19.	B	43.	C	67.	A
20.	D	44.	C	68.	B
21.	D	45.	D	69.	A
22.	C	46.	B	70.	C
23.	A	47.	B	71.	D
24.	C	48.	A	72.	D

Postal Exam 473/473-C
Practice Test Answer Sheet

Tear out or photocopy one two-sided Answer Sheet for each Practice Test. This sheet is similar to the one you will mark at the real exam.

When taking the actual Test 473 or 473-C, you will first fill in the top half of the front side of the Answer Sheet, which asks for information similar to what you provided when applying for the exam. You will mark your answers for Address Checking and Forms Completion on the bottom half of the first side.

On the back side of the Answer Sheet, you will mark your answers for the final two sections of the test: Coding and Memory and Personal Characteristics and Experience Inventory.

For some excellent tips on marking your Answer Sheet, please see **Appendix A: Five Valuable Answer Sheet Marking Strategies** in the back of this book.

Part A: Address Checking

1 (A)(B)(C)(D)	11 (A)(B)(C)(D)	21 (A)(B)(C)(D)	31 (A)(B)(C)(D)	41 (A)(B)(C)(D)	51 (A)(B)(C)(D)
2 (A)(B)(C)(D)	12 (A)(B)(C)(D)	22 (A)(B)(C)(D)	32 (A)(B)(C)(D)	42 (A)(B)(C)(D)	52 (A)(B)(C)(D)
3 (A)(B)(C)(D)	13 (A)(B)(C)(D)	23 (A)(B)(C)(D)	33 (A)(B)(C)(D)	43 (A)(B)(C)(D)	53 (A)(B)(C)(D)
4 (A)(B)(C)(D)	14 (A)(B)(C)(D)	24 (A)(B)(C)(D)	34 (A)(B)(C)(D)	44 (A)(B)(C)(D)	54 (A)(B)(C)(D)
5 (A)(B)(C)(D)	15 (A)(B)(C)(D)	25 (A)(B)(C)(D)	35 (A)(B)(C)(D)	45 (A)(B)(C)(D)	55 (A)(B)(C)(D)
6 (A)(B)(C)(D)	16 (A)(B)(C)(D)	26 (A)(B)(C)(D)	36 (A)(B)(C)(D)	46 (A)(B)(C)(D)	56 (A)(B)(C)(D)
7 (A)(B)(C)(D)	17 (A)(B)(C)(D)	27 (A)(B)(C)(D)	37 (A)(B)(C)(D)	47 (A)(B)(C)(D)	57 (A)(B)(C)(D)
8 (A)(B)(C)(D)	18 (A)(B)(C)(D)	28 (A)(B)(C)(D)	38 (A)(B)(C)(D)	48 (A)(B)(C)(D)	58 (A)(B)(C)(D)
9 (A)(B)(C)(D)	19 (A)(B)(C)(D)	29 (A)(B)(C)(D)	39 (A)(B)(C)(D)	49 (A)(B)(C)(D)	59 (A)(B)(C)(D)
10 (A)(B)(C)(D)	20 (A)(B)(C)(D)	30 (A)(B)(C)(D)	40 (A)(B)(C)(D)	50 (A)(B)(C)(D)	60 (A)(B)(C)(D)

Part B: Forms Completion

1 (A)(B)(C)(D)	6 (A)(B)(C)(D)	11 (A)(B)(C)(D)	16 (A)(B)(C)(D)	21 (A)(B)(C)(D)	26 (A)(B)(C)(D)
2 (A)(B)(C)(D)	7 (A)(B)(C)(D)	12 (A)(B)(C)(D)	17 (A)(B)(C)(D)	22 (A)(B)(C)(D)	27 (A)(B)(C)(D)
3 (A)(B)(C)(D)	8 (A)(B)(C)(D)	13 (A)(B)(C)(D)	18 (A)(B)(C)(D)	23 (A)(B)(C)(D)	28 (A)(B)(C)(D)
4 (A)(B)(C)(D)	9 (A)(B)(C)(D)	14 (A)(B)(C)(D)	19 (A)(B)(C)(D)	24 (A)(B)(C)(D)	29 (A)(B)(C)(D)
5 (A)(B)(C)(D)	10 (A)(B)(C)(D)	15 (A)(B)(C)(D)	20 (A)(B)(C)(D)	25 (A)(B)(C)(D)	30 (A)(B)(C)(D)

continued on other side →

KAPLAN

Part C: Coding and Memory

Coding Section						Memory Section					

Coding Section

1 (A) (B) (C) (D)   13 (A) (B) (C) (D)   25 (A) (B) (C) (D)
2 (A) (B) (C) (D)   14 (A) (B) (C) (D)   26 (A) (B) (C) (D)
3 (A) (B) (C) (D)   15 (A) (B) (C) (D)   27 (A) (B) (C) (D)
4 (A) (B) (C) (D)   16 (A) (B) (C) (D)   28 (A) (B) (C) (D)
5 (A) (B) (C) (D)   17 (A) (B) (C) (D)   29 (A) (B) (C) (D)
6 (A) (B) (C) (D)   18 (A) (B) (C) (D)   30 (A) (B) (C) (D)
7 (A) (B) (C) (D)   19 (A) (B) (C) (D)   31 (A) (B) (C) (D)
8 (A) (B) (C) (D)   20 (A) (B) (C) (D)   32 (A) (B) (C) (D)
9 (A) (B) (C) (D)   21 (A) (B) (C) (D)   33 (A) (B) (C) (D)
10 (A) (B) (C) (D)   22 (A) (B) (C) (D)   34 (A) (B) (C) (D)
11 (A) (B) (C) (D)   23 (A) (B) (C) (D)   35 (A) (B) (C) (D)
12 (A) (B) (C) (D)   24 (A) (B) (C) (D)   36 (A) (B) (C) (D)

Memory Section

37 (A) (B) (C) (D)   49 (A) (B) (C) (D)   61 (A) (B) (C) (D)
38 (A) (B) (C) (D)   50 (A) (B) (C) (D)   62 (A) (B) (C) (D)
39 (A) (B) (C) (D)   51 (A) (B) (C) (D)   63 (A) (B) (C) (D)
40 (A) (B) (C) (D)   52 (A) (B) (C) (D)   64 (A) (B) (C) (D)
41 (A) (B) (C) (D)   53 (A) (B) (C) (D)   65 (A) (B) (C) (D)
42 (A) (B) (C) (D)   54 (A) (B) (C) (D)   66 (A) (B) (C) (D)
43 (A) (B) (C) (D)   55 (A) (B) (C) (D)   67 (A) (B) (C) (D)
44 (A) (B) (C) (D)   56 (A) (B) (C) (D)   68 (A) (B) (C) (D)
45 (A) (B) (C) (D)   57 (A) (B) (C) (D)   69 (A) (B) (C) (D)
46 (A) (B) (C) (D)   58 (A) (B) (C) (D)   70 (A) (B) (C) (D)
47 (A) (B) (C) (D)   59 (A) (B) (C) (D)   71 (A) (B) (C) (D)
48 (A) (B) (C) (D)   60 (A) (B) (C) (D)   72 (A) (B) (C) (D)

Part D: Personal Characteristics and Experience Inventory

[When taking the real Test 473/473-C, you will mark the answers to the 236 questions in this area of the Answer Sheet.]

PRACTICE TEST 6

Part A: Address Checking

Instructions

Part A has 60 questions. You will have 11 minutes to complete this portion of the test. Each item (question) has two side-by-side addresses containing either identical or almost identical information.

You must compare each of the 60 items, decide if they are *exactly* the same or not, and mark the correct answers by blackening the corresponding ovals on your answer sheet. If the two addresses are different, you must decide if there is a difference in only the street address, *or* in the ZIP code only, *or* in both the street address *and* the ZIP code.

There are four answer choices, as you can see from the sample below; and the answer sheet has four ovals for each item, representing those four choices. If the two addresses are the same, darken oval A. If there is a difference in the street address only, darken oval B. If there is a difference in the ZIP code only, darken oval C. And if there is a difference in both the street address and the ZIP code, darken oval D.

A. No Errors	B. Address Only	C. ZIP Code Only	D. Both

Set your timer for exactly 11 minutes. Turn the page when you are ready and begin.

Part A: Address Checking

A. No Errors	B. Address Only	C. ZIP Code Only	D. Both

	Correct List		List to Be Checked	
	Address	ZIP Code	Address	ZIP Code
1.	6768 NW Bruce Pl Racine, WI	77918	6768 NW Bruce Pl Racine, WI	77918
2.	220 Badger Pass Rd Gillette, WY	21054	220 Badger Pass Rd Gillette, WY	21504
3.	164½ Chapman Dr Wheeling, WV	72801	164½ Chapmann Dr Wheeling, WV	78201
4.	22701 Elmrock Av Vancouver, WA	52961	22701 Elmrock Av Vancouver, WA	57961
5.	2947 Kalima Ln Chesapeake, VA	85672	2497 Kalima Ln Chesapeake, VA	85672
6.	374-D Schmidt Ter Winooski, VT	58261	374-D Schmitt Ter Winooski, VT	58261
7.	70182 Psyco Path Provo, UT	29781	70182 Psyco Path Provo, UT	29781
8.	99 S Vittoria Blvd San Antonio, TX	28160	99 S Vittoria Blvd San Antonio, TX	28190
9.	442 Samson Ln Chattanooga, TN	41792	442 Samson Ln Chattanooga, TN	41972
10.	10672 Industrial Way Clemson, SC	62871	10672 Industry Way Clemson, SC	62781
11.	P.O. Box 46792 Deadwood, SD	21092	P.O. Box 46792 Deadwood, SD	21092
12.	289 Jacquelyn Cir Newport, RI	72981	289 Jacquilyn Cir Newport, RI	72981
13.	1667 Engelwood Av NE Titusville, PA	97120	1677 Engelwood Ave NE Titusville, PA	97120
14.	1221 S Baker Cyn Gold Beach, OR	18469	1221 N Baker Cyn Gold Beach, OR	18469
15.	166 Green Pine Wy Guthrie, OK	98210	166 Green Pine Wy Guthrie, OK	92180
16.	826-C Beladre Rd Oxford, OH	61982	826-C Baledre Rd Oxford, OH	61892

A. No Errors	B. Address Only	C. ZIP Code Only	D. Both

Correct List		List to Be Checked	
Address	**ZIP Code**	**Address**	**ZIP Code**
17. 24 Lattimore Dr NE Mandan, ND	16782	24 Lattimore St NE Mandan, ND	16872
18. 822 Sandycreek Ln Asheville, NC	69072	822 Sandycreek Ln Asheville, NC	69072
19. 2719 Colonial Dr White Plains, NY	94671	2179 Colonial Dr White Plains, NY	94671
20. 78916 Grissom St SW Las Cruces, NM	16782	78916 Grissom St SW Las Cruces, NM	16782
21. 186 Los Lobos Ln Asbury Park, NJ	34291	186 Los Lobos Ln Asbury Park, NJ	34921
22. 24-B Salt Air Cir Portsmouth, NH	72962	24-B Salt Air Cir Portsmouth, NH	72692
23. 22861 W Central Av Elko, NV	21726	22861 W Central Av Elko, NV	27126
24. 23741 Hoover Wy Grand Island, NB	21683	24731 Hoover Wy Grand Island, NB	21683
25. 202 E Mariquita St Hannibal, MO	82492	202 E Mariquita Dr Hannibal, MO	84292
26. 126 E 142nd St Anaconda, MT	27962	146 E 142nd St Anaconda, MT	27692
27. 810-A Majorca Hwy Bay St. Louis, MS	13904	810-A Majorca Hwy Bay St. Louis, MS	13904
28. 667 Rosehedge Dr Saint Cloud, MN	35781	667 Rosehedge Dr Saint Cloud, MN	35781
29. 7819 SW Yorktown Av Dearborn, MI	17203	7819 NW Yorktown Av Dearborn, MI	17203
30. P O Box 16683 Marlborough, MA	82561	P O Box 16863 Marlborough, MA	82561
31. 1510 SE 51st St Laurel, MD	92701	1510 SE 51st St Laurel, MD	92701
32. 2281 Wyandote Ln Bangor, ME	85703	2281 Wyandote Ln Bangor, ME	87503
33. 1234 ½ Zig Zag Way Alexandria, LA	27803-7245	1234 ½ Zig Zag Way Alexandria, LA	27308-7245
34. 223 Stage Coach Rd Lexington, KY	73692	223 Stage Coach Ln Lexington, KY	76932

| A. No Errors | B. Address Only | C. ZIP Code Only | D. Both |

| Correct List | | List to Be Checked | |
Address	ZIP Code	Address	ZIP Code
35. P.O. Box 14571 Dodge City, KS	14782	P.O. Box 15471 Dodge City, KS	14872
36. 17181 Stirrup Ct Fort Dodge, IA	31684	17871 Stirrup Ct Fort Dodge, IA	31864
37. 781-A W Bamboo St Gary, IN	65871	781-A W Bamboo St Gary, IN	65871
38. 81974 Emery Ave Chicago Heights, IL	22861	81974 Emery Ave Chicago Heights, IL	22861
39. 1671 E Lincoln Pl Twin Falls, ID	85631	1761 E Lincoln Pl Twin Falls, ID	85631
40. 225 ¼ W Southern Ln Hilo, HI	22689	225 ½ W Southern Ln Hilo, HI	22689
41. 122 N 122nd Pl Savannah, GA	93624	122 N 122nd Pl Savannah, GA	98624
42. 4229 Lorca Way SE Fort Walton Beach, FL	78204	4299 Lorca Way SE Fort Walton Beach, FL	78024
43. 2006 K St NW Washingon, DC	57928	2006 K St NW Washington, DC	59278
44. 2525 Hercules Hwy Seaford, DE	99372	2525 Hercules Hwy Seaford, DE	99732
45. 705 S Jardines Ave Santa Barbara, CA	40792	705 S Jardines Ave Santa Barbara, CA	40792
46. 333 Quiet Path New Britain, CT	70462	333 Quiet Path New Britain, CT	70642
47. 2278 Pullman Pl Vail, CO	35201	2278 Pulmann Pl Vail, CO	35201
48. 6675 Jacalyne Ln Hope, AR	60382	6775 Jacalyne Ln Hope, AR	60382
49. 2250 Gaslight Dr Nogales, AZ	80247	2550 Gaslight Dr Nogales, AZ	80427
50. 80426 Dorsett Blvd Anniston, AL	65903	80426 Dorsset Blvd Anniston, AL	65093
51. 2271-E Dapple Grey Dr Anchorage, AK	32723	2271-E Dapple Grey Dr Anchorage, AK	32372
52. 8824 Butterfield St Rome, GA	40682-2574	8824 Butterfield St Rome, GA	40682-2574

| A. No Errors | B. Address Only | C. ZIP Code Only | D. Both |

Correct List		**List to Be Checked**	
Address	**ZIP Code**	**Address**	**ZIP Code**
53. 2801 Gettysburg Trace Alfred, ME	82107	2801 Gettysburg Trace Alfred, ME	82107
54. 19395 W Liberty Blvd Bethesda, MD	85692	19395 W Liberty Blvd Bethesda, MD	85962
55. P.O. Box 22671 St. Louis, MO	29715	P.O. Box 22671 St. Louis, MO	29175
56. 295-B W 53rd St Brownsville, TX	20503	295-D W 53rd St Brownsville, TX	20503
57. 6294 125th Ave NW Saint Paul, MN	17394	6294 125th Ave SW Saint Paul, MN	19374
58. 2424 Los Coyotes Ave San Jose, CA	68275	2424 Los Coyotes Ave San Jose, CA	68275
59. 8192 SW California Ln Moses Lake, WA	27901-3185	8192 SW California Ln Moses Lake, WA	27901-3815

60. 22591 Linear Dr
Truth or
    Consequences, NM
	26195	22591 Linear Dr
		Truth or
		    Consequences, NM
			26195

This is the end of Part A: Address Checking Section, Practice Test 6.

Part B: Forms Completion

Part B consists of 30 questions that test your ability to identify the information needed to correctly complete various U.S. Postal Service forms. You will be shown 5 different forms, each followed by 6 questions.

Set your timer for exactly 15 minutes. Turn the page and begin when you are ready.

Part B: Forms Completion

Certificate of Bulk Mailing

Fee for Certificate	1. [Current Rate Chart Here]	2. Meter stamp or postage stamps to be affixed here, and cancelled by postmarking with date.
Up to 1,000 pieces		
For each additional 1,000 pieces or fraction thereof		

3a. Number of indentical pieces	3b. Class of mail	3c. Postage on each	3d. Number of pieces per lb.	3e. Total number of lbs.	3f. Total postage paid	3g. Fee paid

Postmaster's Certificate: I hereby certify that the above-described mailing has been received and number of pieces and postage verified.

4. Signature and Date _____

Part B: Forms Completion

1. Which of these would be an acceptable entry for Box 3a?
   A. 1,300
   B. Jasper Mailing Service
   C. 54312-0094
   D. 9770 Culver Blvd.

2. Where would the class of mail be indicated?
   A. Box 2
   B. Box 3a
   C. Box 3b
   D. Box 3e

3. The postage on each item is $0.32. Where would you indicate this amount?
   A. Box 1
   B. Box 3c
   C. Box 3f
   D. Line 4

4. Postage stamps should be affixed where on this form?
   A. Box 1
   B. Box 2
   C. Box 3g
   D. Box 4

5. The manager of Ace Bulk Mailing Service is mailing 3,545 pieces of mail. Where should she sign this form?
   A. Box 1
   B. Box 2
   C. Line 4
   D. None of the above

6. Where would you indicate the number of identical pieces?
   A. Box 3a
   B. Box 3d
   C. Box 3a and Box 3d
   D. None of the above

Part B: Forms Completion

Customs Declaration and Dispatch Note

From						
Sender's Name						
Business						
Street						
City	State	ZIP Code®				
Country						

To			
Addressee's Name			
Business			
Street			
Postcode	City		
Country			

Detailed Description of Contents (1)	Qty. (2)	Net Weight (3) lb.　oz.	Value (US $) (5)	For Commercial Senders Only	
				HS tariff number (7)	Country of origin of goods (8)

Check One ☐ Airmail/Priority ☐ Surface/Nonpriority	Total Gross Wt. (4)	Total Value (6)	Postage and Fees (9)

Check One (10) ☐ Gift　☐ Commercial sample　☐ Other
☐ Documents　☐ Returned goods　Explanation:

Comments (11) *(e.g., goods subject to quarantine, sanitary/phytosanitary inspection, or other restrictions)*

License Number(s) (12)	Certificate Number(s) (13)	Invoice Number (14)

Sender's Instructions in Case of Nondelivery (16)　Mailing Office Date Stamp
☐ Treat as Abandoned
☐ Return to Sender -
NOTE: Item subject to return charges at sender's expense.
☐ Redirect to Address Below:

I certify that the particulars given in this customs declaration are correct and that this item does not contain any dangerous article prohibited by legislation or by postal or customs regulations.

Date and sender's signature (15)

Part B: Forms Completion

7. Where would you indicate that documents are being mailed?
   A. Box 1
   B. Box 10
   C. Box 1 and Box 10
   D. Box 11

8. Lara McKinney is the sender. Rob Tarik is the addressee. Where should Rob Tarik sign the form?
   A. In the FROM box
   B. In the TO box
   C. Box 15
   D. Rob Tarik is not supposed to sign this form.

9. Which box or boxes could correctly contain dollar amounts?
   A. Box 9
   B. Boxes 5 and 6
   C. Boxes 5, 6, and 9
   D. Boxes 5, 6, 9, and 10

10. Which of the following would be an appropriate entry for Box 1?
    A. Wool fishermen's sweaters
    B. Rev. Dr. Jim Nelson
    C. December 21, 2006
    D. 37 lb, 4 oz

11. In which of these would a check mark be appropriate?
    A. Box 10
    B. Box 16
    C. Both Box 10 and Box 15
    D. Both Box 10 and Box 16

12. The package contains fruit from Brazil. How would you indicate that the contents of the package are subject to quarantine?
    A. Write "Goods subject to quarantine" in Box 1
    B. Write "Goods subject to quarantine" in Box 11
    C. Check the "Commercial sample" box
    D. Check the "Goods subject to quarantine" box

Part B: Forms Completion

Delivery Type File Order Form

Customer Shipping Information		
1. Attention:		
2. Company:		
3a. Street Address, PO Box, Rural Hwy Contract Route and Box #:		**3b.** Apt/Suite #:
4a. City and State:		**4b.** ZIP + 4 :
5a. Foreign Country (*If applicable*):		**5b.** Foreign Postal Code (*If applicable*):
6a. Phone Number:	**6b.** FAX Number:	**6c.** Email Address:

Payment Method	
☐ Check ☐ Money Order ☐ Visa ☐ MasterCard ☐ American Express	Credit Card #: _____ Card Exp. Date: _____ Signature: _____

Part B: Forms Completion

13. The customer's FAX number is 312-555-4399. Where would you write this information?
- A. Box 4b
- B. Box 6a
- C. Box 6b
- D. Box 6c

14. Which of the following is an appropriate entry for Box 6c?
- A. Bentbacktulip@axl.com
- B. www.usps.com
- C. $187.15
- D. 07/18/06

15. What payment options are listed on this form?
- A. Cash only
- B. Check or money order only
- C. Check, money order, or credit card
- D. Cash, check, money order, or credit card

16. Which of these would be an acceptable entry for Box 4a?
- A. Park Ridge, IL 60068-4216
- B. Park Ridge, IL
- C. Illinois
- D. United States

17. Which of these would be an acceptable entry for Box 2?
- A. La Crescenta, WA
- B. Maggie Hoyt
- C. Money order
- D. Disco Collectibles Co. Inc.

18. What information is requested if the customer is using a credit card for payment?
- A. Credit card type, number, and customer's signature
- B. Credit card type, number, expiration date, and customer's signature
- C. Credit card type, number, expiration date, and address
- D. All of the above

Part B: Forms Completion

Mail Forwarding Change of Address Order

		OFFICIAL USE ONLY
Please PRINT Items 1–10 in blue or black ink. Your signature is required in Item 9.		Zone/Route ID No.
1. Change of Address for: (Read Attached Inastructions) ☐ Individual (#5) ☐ Entire Family (#5) ☐ Business (#6)	2. Is This Move Temporary? ☐ Yes ☐ No	Date Entered on Form 3982 M M D D Y Y
3. Start Date:	4. If TEMPORARY move, print date to discontinue forwarding:	Expiration Date M M D D Y Y
5. LAST Name & Jr./Sr./etc.		Clerk/Carrier Endorsement
5b. FIRST Name and MI		
6. If BUSINESS Move, Print Business Name		
PRINT OLD MAILING ADDRESS BELOW: HOUSE/BUILDING NUMBER AND STREET NAME (INCLUDE ST., AVE., CT., ETC.) OR P.O. BOX		
7a. OLD Mailing Address		
7a. OLD APT or Suite	7b. For Puerto Rico Only: If address is in PR, print urbanization name, if appropriate	
7c. OLD CITY		7d. State / 7e. ZIP
8a. NEW Mailing Address	8b. For Puerto Rico Only: If address is in PR, print urbanization name, if appropriate	
8c. NEW CITY		8d. State / 8e. ZIP
9. Print and Sign Name (see conditions on reverse) ➤ Print: Sign:	10. Date Signed:	

Part B: Forms Completion

19. The new city is Enterprise. Where should this be entered?
    A. Box 7c
    B. Box 8a
    C. Box 8b
    D. Box 8c

20. Where could the postal abbreviation for Nevada (NV) be entered?
    A. Box 4
    B. Box 7d
    C. Box 8d
    D. Box 7d and Box 8d

21. What would be an acceptable entry for Box 5a?
    A. Foxworthy, Jr.
    B. Helen Gray
    C. Star Charts Ltd.
    D. Austin, TX

22. What would be an acceptable entry for Box 6?
    A. Foxworthy, Jr
    B. Helen Gray
    C. Star Charts Ltd.
    D. Austin, TX

23. How would you indicate that the change of address is for the entire family?
    A. A signature in Box 9
    B. A check mark in Box 1
    C. A check mark in Box 2
    D. Initials in the date stamp

24. How many places on this form could a date be appropriately entered?
    A. Two
    B. Three
    C. Five
    D. Six

Part B: Forms Completion

Domestic Claim or Registered Mail Inquiry

Mailer Information	Addressee Information
1a. Name:	2a. Name:
1b. Business or Company Name:	2b. Business or Company Name:
1c. No. and Street, Apt/Suite:	2c. No. and Street, Apt/Suite:
1d. City, State, ZIP + 4:	2d. City, State, ZIP + 4:
1e. Telephone *(with area code):*	2e. Telephone *(with area code):*

3. Payment Assignment	4. Description of Lost or Damaged Article(s) (Add Extra Sheets as Needed)			
3a. Who is to receive payment? *(Check one)*	Item	Description	Purchase Date	Value
☐ Mailer	A	4a.		
☐ Addressee	B	4b.		
	C	4c.		
5a. COD Amount to be remitted to sender: $ _____	5b. Total amount claimed for all articles: $ _____			

Certification and Signature		
6a. Customer submitting claim: ☐ Mailer ☐ Addressee	6b. Customer Signature:	6c. Date Signed:

Part B: Forms Completion

25. If a COD amount is to be remitted to the sender, where would this be indicated?
    A. Box 3a
    B. Box 5a
    C. Box 5b
    D. None of the above

26. For which of these would "Woodbury, CT 06798-1123" be an acceptable entry?
    A. Box 1d
    B. Box 2d
    C. Box 1d and Box 2d
    D. There is no request for an address on this form.

27. Carla Saldana is the addressee receiving payment of $230. How would you indicate that Carla is to receive payment?
    A. Carla's name in Box 2a
    B. Carla's address in Boxes 2b, 2c, and 2d
    C. A check mark in Box 3a
    D. Carla's signature in Box 6b

28. Which of the following would be an acceptable entry in Box 2e?
    A. 845-555-1826
    B. Moscow
    C. 08-29-07
    D. $79.78

29. Damaged Item B was a broken Chinese vase. Where would you put its description?
    A. Line 3a
    B. Line 4a
    C. Line 4b
    D. Line 5c

30. For which of these would "Dr. Ayisha Melville" be an acceptable entry?
    A. Box 1b
    B. Box 1c
    C. Box 5a
    D. None of the above

This is the end of Part B: Forms Completion, Practice Test 6.

Part C: Coding and Memory

Overview

In Part C you will need to work quickly and accurately, using one Coding Guide to answer questions in two separate sections, the Coding Section and the Memory Section.

Prior to the scored segments of both the Coding Section and the Memory Section, there are practice segments. This test will follow the same format.

The Coding Guide that is used throughout Part C consists of four delivery routes. Three of the routes have two or three address ranges associated with them, and the last route covers any address not within the other three routes.

Each question (item) in both the Coding Section and the Memory Section consists of an address. Your job is to determine which of the four routes a given address belongs to and to mark your answer sheet accordingly.

In the Coding Section you may use the Coding Guide to determine the correct route for each address. In the Memory Section you will see exactly the same type of questions that are in the Coding Section, but you will no longer be able to look at the Coding Guide. Rather, you must determine which of the four routes an address belongs to, using only your memory of the Coding Guide.

The scored portion of the Coding Section has 36 questions, and you have 6 minutes to answer them. Prior to the scored portion, you will have two opportunities to practice using the Coding Guide.

The scored portion of the Memory Section also has 36 questions and 7 minutes to answer them. It also provides you with two opportunities to study and memorize the Coding Guide, as well as a chance to practice answering questions without using the Coding Guide.

Part C: Coding Section

Part 1: Sample Questions

Instructions   Answering the questions on the following pages will familiarize you with the format and timing of the questions in Part C: Coding Section. You will have 3½ minutes to answer 12 questions, using the Coding Guide displayed opposite the questions.

Mark your answers in the sample ovals and check your answers using the correct answers shown at the bottom of the same page.

Set your timer for 3½ minutes and turn the page when you are ready to begin.

Part C: Coding Section

Coding Guide	
Address Range	**Delivery Route**
277–799 Daphne Dr 74–601 NW 172nd Pl 3101–4200 Dilbert Ln	A
4500–5651 Hillhurst 9920–10410 Plainview Rd	B
1478–2010 Los Feliz Blvd 935–1389 S San Fernando 201–555 Rural Route 2	C
Any mail that is not found in one of the above address ranges	D

Part C: Coding Section

Exercise 1: Sample Questions

	Address	Delivery Route			
1.	10204 Plainview Rd	(A)	(B)	(C)	(D)
2.	426 Rural Route 2	(A)	(B)	(C)	(D)
3.	971 San Fernando	(A)	(B)	(C)	(D)
4.	200 Rural Route 2	(A)	(B)	(C)	(D)
5.	801 Daphne Dr	(A)	(B)	(C)	(D)
6.	599 NW 172nd Pl	(A)	(B)	(C)	(D)
7.	4701 Hillhurst	(A)	(B)	(C)	(D)
8.	1520 Los Feliz Blvd	(A)	(B)	(C)	(D)
9.	3856 Dilbert Ln	(A)	(B)	(C)	(D)
10.	10112 Planeview Rd	(A)	(B)	(C)	(D)
11.	332 NW 172nd Pl	(A)	(B)	(C)	(D)
12.	1099 S San Fernando	(A)	(B)	(C)	(D)

Answers

1. B
2. C
3. C
4. D
5. A
6. A
7. B
8. C
9. A
10. D
11. A
12. C

Part C: Coding Section

Coding Practice Test 6

Instructions   This section follows the format of Postal Exam 473. There are 36 questions, and you will have 6 minutes to answer them. Each page of questions is displayed opposite the Coding Guide, which you may use to answer the questions.

You will score this section and use it to help determine your score on this practice test. Mark your answers on your Practice Test 6 Answer Sheet in the Coding Section of Part C.

Set your timer for 6 minutes and turn the page when you are ready to begin.

Coding Guide	
Address Range	**Delivery Route**
277–799 Daphne Dr 74–601 NW 172nd Pl 3101–4200 Dilbert Ln	A
4500–5651 Hillhurst 9920--0410 Plainview Rd	B
1478–2010 Los Feliz Blvd 935–1389 S San Fernando 201–555 Rural Route 2	C
Any mail that is not found in one of the above address ranges	D

Coding Section: Practice Test 6

Questions

	Address	Delivery Route			
1.	4199 Dilbert Ln	(A)	(B)	(C)	(D)
2.	5510 Hillhurst	(A)	(B)	(C)	(D)
3.	441 Rural Route 2	(A)	(B)	(C)	(D)
4.	4551 Hillview	(A)	(B)	(C)	(D)
5.	5610 Hillhurst	(A)	(B)	(C)	(D)
6.	1010 S San Fernando	(A)	(B)	(C)	(D)
7.	2100 Los Feliz Blvd	(A)	(B)	(C)	(D)
8.	593 NW 172nd Pl	(A)	(B)	(C)	(D)
9.	554 Rural Route 2	(A)	(B)	(C)	(D)
10.	3247 Dilbert Ln	(A)	(B)	(C)	(D)
11.	526 Daphne Dr	(A)	(B)	(C)	(D)
12.	289 NW 172nd Pl	(A)	(B)	(C)	(D)
13.	1953 Los Feliz Blvd	(A)	(B)	(C)	(D)
14.	1274 N San Fernando	(A)	(B)	(C)	(D)
15.	5107 Hillhurst	(A)	(B)	(C)	(D)
16.	10101 Plainview Rd	(A)	(B)	(C)	(D)
17.	4126 Dilbert Ln	(A)	(B)	(C)	(D)
18.	1111 S San Fernando	(A)	(B)	(C)	(D)
19.	443 Rural Route 4	(A)	(B)	(C)	(D)

Coding Guide	
Address Range	**Delivery Route**
277–799 Daphne Dr 74–601 NW 172nd Pl 3101–4200 Dilbert Ln	A
4500–5651 Hillhurst 9920–10410 Plainview Rd	B
1478–2010 Los Feliz Blvd 935–1389 S San Fernando 201–555 Rural Route 2	C
Any mail that is not found in one of the above address ranges	D

20.	600 NW 172nd Pl	Ⓐ	Ⓑ	Ⓒ	Ⓓ
21.	601-A Daphne Dr	Ⓐ	Ⓑ	Ⓒ	Ⓓ
22.	1536 Los Feliz Blvd	Ⓐ	Ⓑ	Ⓒ	Ⓓ
23.	9931 Plainview Rd	Ⓐ	Ⓑ	Ⓒ	Ⓓ
24.	1210 S San Fernando	Ⓐ	Ⓑ	Ⓒ	Ⓓ
25.	1874 Los Feliz Blvd	Ⓐ	Ⓑ	Ⓒ	Ⓓ
26.	298 Rural Route 2	Ⓐ	Ⓑ	Ⓒ	Ⓓ
27.	4100 Dilbert Ln	Ⓐ	Ⓑ	Ⓒ	Ⓓ
28.	601 Daphne Ave	Ⓐ	Ⓑ	Ⓒ	Ⓓ
29.	4750 Hillhurst	Ⓐ	Ⓑ	Ⓒ	Ⓓ
30.	10209 Plainview Rd	Ⓐ	Ⓑ	Ⓒ	Ⓓ
31.	3566 Dilbert Ln	Ⓐ	Ⓑ	Ⓒ	Ⓓ
32.	512 NW 172nd Pl	Ⓐ	Ⓑ	Ⓒ	Ⓓ
33.	768 Daphne Dr	Ⓐ	Ⓑ	Ⓒ	Ⓓ
34.	310 Rural Route 2	Ⓐ	Ⓑ	Ⓒ	Ⓓ
35.	935 S San Fernando	Ⓐ	Ⓑ	Ⓒ	Ⓓ
36.	3010 Dilbert Ln	Ⓐ	Ⓑ	Ⓒ	Ⓓ

This is the end of Part C: Coding Section, Practice Test 6.

Part C: Memory Section

Overview

There are four divisions in Part C: Memory Section. They are

1. a 3-minute period for studying the Coding Guide;
2. a 90-second nonscored practice, in which you answer 8 questions without using the Coding Guide;
3. a 5-minute period for studying the Coding Guide; and
4. a scored test, consisting of 36 questions, timed for 7 minutes.

During the two study periods there are no questions to answer; you are memorizing the Coding Guide. Section 2 is a timed practice test, with 8 questions to answer in 90 seconds, and a sample answer sheet. Section 4 is the actual test. Use the Practice Test 6 answer sheet to mark your answers. They will be scored.

Memory Section: Part 1

Instructions

Part 1 of the Memory Section is a study period. Use it to memorize the Coding Guide. There are no questions to answer during the 3-minute study period.

Set your timer for 3 minutes, and when you are ready to begin, turn the page.

Memory Section: Part 1

Coding Guide	
Address Range	**Delivery Route**
277–799 Daphne Dr 74–601 NW 172nd Pl 3101–4200 Dilbert Ln	A
4500–5651 Hillhurst 9920–10410 Plainview Rd	B
1478–2010 Los Feliz Blvd 935–1389 S San Fernando 201–555 Rural Route 2	C
Any mail that is not found in one of the above address ranges	D

Memory Section: Part 2

Instructions

In Part 2 of the Memory Section you will practice answering questions using your memory of the Coding Guide (see p. 283), which will not be shown. This is only a practice exercise; it will not be scored.

Following the 8 questions is a sample answer sheet that you will use to mark your answers. At the bottom of the page is the answer key for the sample questions.

Set your timer for 90 seconds; when you are ready, you may begin.

Memory Section: Part 2

	Address	Delivery Route			
1.	345 Rural Route 2	(A)	(B)	(C)	(D)
2.	1229 S San Fernando	(A)	(B)	(C)	(D)
3.	485 Daphne Dr	(A)	(B)	(C)	(D)
4.	9999 Plainview Rd	(A)	(B)	(C)	(D)
5.	1479 S San Fernando	(A)	(B)	(C)	(D)
6.	4760 Hillhurst	(A)	(B)	(C)	(D)
7.	600 NW 172nd Pl	(A)	(B)	(C)	(D)
8.	312 Daphne Dr	(A)	(B)	(C)	(D)

Answers

1. C
2. C
3. A
4. B
5. D
6. B
7. A
8. A

Memory Section: Part 3

Instructions

Part 3 of the Memory Section is a 5-minute study period. This is your final preparation period for the scored Memory test. Use it to finish memorizing the Coding Guide. As in Part 1 of this section, there are no questions to answer. Do not make marks of any kind during this study period.

Set your timer for 5 minutes, and when you are ready, turn the page and begin.

Memory Section: Part 3

Coding Guide	
Address Range	**Delivery Route**
277–799 Daphne Dr 74–601 NW 172nd Pl 3101–4200 Dilbert Ln	A
4500–5651 Hillhurst 9920–10410 Plainview Rd	B
1478–2010 Los Feliz Blvd 935–1389 S San Fernando 201–555 Rural Route 2	C
Any mail that is not found in one of the above address ranges	D

Memory Section: Part 4

Instructions

Part 4 of the Memory Section is the scored Memory test. You will have 7 minutes to answer the 36 questions, without using the Coding Guide. You must answer the questions from memory.

Mark your answers to these 36 questions on the Practice Test 6 Answer Sheet, using lines 37–72 of Part C: Coding and Memory. When you have finished, it is time to score the exam.

Set your timer for 7 minutes, and when you are ready, begin.

Memory Section: Practice Test 6

Questions

	Address	Delivery Route			
37.	791 Daphne Ln	Ⓐ	Ⓑ	Ⓒ	Ⓓ
38.	5562 Hillhurst	Ⓐ	Ⓑ	Ⓒ	Ⓓ
39.	9940 Plainview	Ⓐ	Ⓑ	Ⓒ	Ⓓ
40.	509 Rural Route 2	Ⓐ	Ⓑ	Ⓒ	Ⓓ
41.	4101 Dilbert Ln	Ⓐ	Ⓑ	Ⓒ	Ⓓ
42.	783 Daphne Dr	Ⓐ	Ⓑ	Ⓒ	Ⓓ
43.	5367 Hillburst	Ⓐ	Ⓑ	Ⓒ	Ⓓ
44.	496 Rural Route 2	Ⓐ	Ⓑ	Ⓒ	Ⓓ
45.	1486 Los Feliz Blvd	Ⓐ	Ⓑ	Ⓒ	Ⓓ
46.	10408 Plainview Rd	Ⓐ	Ⓑ	Ⓒ	Ⓓ
47.	713 Daphne Dr	Ⓐ	Ⓑ	Ⓒ	Ⓓ
48.	4201 Dilbert Ln	Ⓐ	Ⓑ	Ⓒ	Ⓓ
49.	525 NW 172nd Pl	Ⓐ	Ⓑ	Ⓒ	Ⓓ
50.	3629 Dilbert Ln	Ⓐ	Ⓑ	Ⓒ	Ⓓ
51.	279 Daphne Dr	Ⓐ	Ⓑ	Ⓒ	Ⓓ
52.	543 Rural Route 2	Ⓐ	Ⓑ	Ⓒ	Ⓓ
53.	5050 Hillhurst	Ⓐ	Ⓑ	Ⓒ	Ⓓ
54.	2001 Los Feliz Blvd	Ⓐ	Ⓑ	Ⓒ	Ⓓ
55.	213 Rural Route 2	Ⓐ	Ⓑ	Ⓒ	Ⓓ

56.	976 S San Fernando	Ⓐ Ⓑ Ⓒ Ⓓ
57.	9929 Plainview Rd	Ⓐ Ⓑ Ⓒ Ⓓ
58.	729 Daphne Dr	Ⓐ Ⓑ Ⓒ Ⓓ
59.	3888 Dilbert Ln	Ⓐ Ⓑ Ⓒ Ⓓ
60.	521 SW 172nd Pl	Ⓐ Ⓑ Ⓒ Ⓓ
61.	4002 Dilbert Ln	Ⓐ Ⓑ Ⓒ Ⓓ
62.	456 Rural Route 2	Ⓐ Ⓑ Ⓒ Ⓓ
63.	4600 Hillhurst	Ⓐ Ⓑ Ⓒ Ⓓ
64.	10402 Plainview Rd	Ⓐ Ⓑ Ⓒ Ⓓ
65.	4100 Dilbert Pl	Ⓐ Ⓑ Ⓒ Ⓓ
66.	953 S San Fernando	Ⓐ Ⓑ Ⓒ Ⓓ
67.	698 Daphne Dr	Ⓐ Ⓑ Ⓒ Ⓓ
68.	502 NW 172nd Pl	Ⓐ Ⓑ Ⓒ Ⓓ
69.	1989 Los Feliz Blvd	Ⓐ Ⓑ Ⓒ Ⓓ
70.	4752 Hillhurst	Ⓐ Ⓑ Ⓒ Ⓓ
71.	445 Rural Route 3	Ⓐ Ⓑ Ⓒ Ⓓ
72.	4121 Dilbert Ln	Ⓐ Ⓑ Ⓒ Ⓓ

This is the end of Part C: Memory Section, Practice Test 6.

Part D: Personal Characteristics and Experience Inventory

As explained earlier, it is not possible to prepare for or practice the 236 job-related characteristics and experience questions in Part D. Therefore, no test items are included in this practice exam. For examples, please see Chapters 2 and 6.

Remember, there are no right or wrong answers in this section of Postal Test 473/473-C. Moreover, the USPS does not reveal how it evaluates the highly personal responses to Part D, nor how it weighs this part.

Feel confident that if you select the one response for each statement/question that best reflects your own personality, experience, and work ethics, you will be honestly representing yourself.

ANSWER KEY FOR PRACTICE TEST 6

Part A: Address Checking

1.	A	21.	C	41.	C
2.	C	22.	C	42.	D
3.	D	23.	C	43.	C
4.	C	24.	B	44.	C
5.	B	25.	D	45.	A
6.	B	26.	D	46.	C
7.	A	27.	A	47.	B
8.	C	28.	A	48.	B
9.	C	29.	B	49.	D
10.	D	30.	B	50.	D
11.	A	31.	A	51.	C
12.	B	32.	C	52.	A
13.	B	33.	C	53.	A
14.	B	34.	D	54.	C
15.	C	35.	D	55.	C
16.	D	36.	D	56.	B
17.	D	37.	A	57.	D
18.	A	38.	A	58.	A
19.	B	39.	B	59.	C
20.	A	40.	B	60.	A

KAPLAN

Part B: Forms Completion

1.	A	11.	D	21.	A
2.	C	12.	B	22.	C
3.	B	13.	C	23.	B
4.	B	14.	A	24.	C
5.	D	15.	C	25.	B
6.	A	16.	B	26.	C
7.	C	17.	D	27.	C
8.	D	18.	B	28.	A
9.	C	19.	D	29.	C
10.	A	20.	D	30.	D

Part C: Coding and Memory

1.	A	25.	C	49.	A
2.	B	26.	C	50.	A
3.	C	27.	A	51.	A
4.	D	28.	D	52.	C
5.	B	29.	B	53.	B
6.	C	30.	B	54.	C
7.	C	31.	A	55.	C
8.	A	32.	A	56.	C
9.	D	33.	A	57.	B
10.	A	34.	C	58.	A
11.	A	35.	C	59.	A
12.	A	36.	D	60.	D
13.	C	37.	D	61.	A
14.	D	38.	B	62.	C
15.	B	39.	B	63.	B
16.	B	40.	C	64.	B
17.	A	41.	A	65.	D
18.	C	42.	A	66.	C
19.	D	43.	D	67.	A
20.	A	44.	C	68.	A
21.	A	45.	C	69.	C
22.	C	46.	B	70.	B
23.	B	47.	A	71.	D
24.	C	48.	D	72.	A

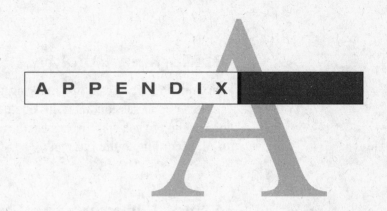
Five Valuable Answer Sheet Marking Strategies

Speed is a key ingredient in taking U.S. Postal Exam 473. To improve your speed, consider following these five valuable tips for answer sheet marking.

1. Buying Your Pencil

Bring pencils, as instructed in your scheduling packet, even though your test site will have pencils available. Some test-takers prefer a #2 pencil with oversized lead that leaves a broader mark. These can be purchased at art and office supply stores and in the stationery sections of chain stores and supermarkets. Practice with several kinds of #2 pencils, including round-shaped and hexagonal-shaped, and see which your hand prefers.

2. Holding Your Pencil

Experiment with holding your pencil in a position that is more horizontal than vertical. Some test-takers poise an index finger on top and near the point of the pencil, thereby using the broader side of the lead. If you want a broader, flatter lead that will fill the answer bubble faster, use one side of the pencil's point until it flattens; for example, hold your pencil with the writing side on the pencil always down. Try different angles, edges, and points until you are both comfortable and speedy!

3. Marking Quickly

On your Practice Tests, try marking the answer sheets with fast back-and-forth strokes in one section and with one or two revolutions of the dulled pencil point on another, to see what works best for you. Your goal is to darken over half of the oval, according to the Exam 473/473-C instructions.

4. Not Filling up the Entire Oval

Use just one or two strokes of your dulled pencil to fill as much as you can (and at least half) of the answer bubble. Do not take the time to completely fill in the oval, but be sure that you are not outside the border of each oval or the computer that scores the answer sheet will not be able to register your marks.

5. Making Notes

Unless instructed otherwise for a specific part—such as the two memory sections of Part C—you may make notes or write anything anywhere *in the test booklet*. Do not make notes or any random marks, however, *on the answer sheet*. The only marks on your answer sheet should be where you have filled in the ovals of your answer choices.

Information for Veterans

Eligible Veterans May Qualify for Special Testing, Scoring, and Hiring Benefits to Become a Postal Worker

Note: The following USPS benefits and requirements may be revised from time to time, particularly as United States military personnel become involved in armed conflicts. To take advantage of these benefits or for additional information, veterans should contact their nearest Postal District Office.

Special Testing

- Rather than waiting for the next public exam, all veterans may apply for exams within 120 days before or after their discharge date.
- Rather than waiting for the next public exam, eligible 10-point veterans may apply once at any time for any or all exams at any or all installations.

Special Scoring with Preference Points

Eligible veterans may qualify to have five or ten preference points added to their raw test scores. It is possible for an eligible veteran to score over 100 on an exam after adding preference points.

Five Points (Tentative) may be awarded to a veteran who was separated under honorable conditions, is not disabled, and who meets one or more of the following criteria:

- Served active duty in pre-World War II campaign or during World War II (12/7/41–4/28/52)
- Served active duty during the period beginning 4/28/52 and ending 7/1/55
- Served active duty for more than 180 consecutive days, other than for training, any part of which occurred between 2/1/55 and 10/14/76
- Began active duty after 10/14/76 and before 9/8/80 and served in a campaign or expedition for which a campaign badge is authorized
- Enlisted after 9/7/80 or entered active duty through other means after 10/14/82 and completed 24 months of continuous service or the full period for which called to active duty and served in a campaign or expedition for which a campaign badge is authorized
- Enlisted after 9/7/80 or entered active duty through means other than enlistment after 10/14/82 and completed 24 months of continuous service or the full period for which called to active duty and served active duty during the period beginning 8/2/90 and ending 1/2/92
- Served in a campaign or expedition for which a campaign badge is authorized and was discharged early under 10 U.S.C. 1171 or for hardship under 10 U.S.C. 1173

Ten Points—Compensable (Less than 30 percent) may be awarded to a veteran who was separated under honorable conditions and has a service-connected disability that is at least 10 percent but less than 30 percent compensable.

Ten Points—Compensable (30 percent or more) may be awarded to a veteran who was separated under honorable conditions and has a service-connected disability that is 30 percent or more compensable.

Ten Points (Other) 10 preference points may be awarded to the following:

- Veterans who were awarded the Purple Heart
- Veterans who receive compensation or pension from the Department of Veterans Affairs or disability retired pay from the Armed Forces
- Veterans who have a service-connected disability that is not compensable or that is less that 10 percent compensable

- The unremarried widow or widower of an honorably separated veteran, provided the deceased veteran served in active duty during a war or died while in the Armed Forces
- Spouses of certain veterans with a service-connected disability
- Mothers of certain deceased or disabled veterans

Special Hiring

In some cases, an eligible ten-point veteran must be hired before a non-veteran, even if the non-veteran has a higher exam score.